YOU CAN HAVE IT ALL AND OTHER PHONY PROMISES

YOU CAN HAVE IT ALL
AND OTHER PHONY PROMISES

DALE AND SANDY LARSEN

VICTOR BOOKS®
A DIVISION OF SCRIPTURE PRESS PUBLICATIONS INC.
USA CANADA ENGLAND

You Can Have It All and Other Phony Promises contrasts the Bible's answers with the messages teenagers are bombarded with in their everyday lives. Student activity booklets (Rip-Off Sheets) and a leader's guide with visual aids (SonPower Multiuse Transparency Masters) are available from your local Christian bookstore or from the publisher.

Library of Congress Catalog Card Number: 88-60222

ISBN: 0-89693-586-8

Recommended Dewey Decimal Classification: 248.83
Suggested Subject Heading: YOUTH—RELIGIOUS LIFE

Printed in the United States of America.

CONTENTS

MESSAGE ONE
You Can Have It All (and You Deserve It!)

MESSAGE TWO
Look and See, Here's What You Should Be

MESSAGE THREE
It's All within You—Just Look inside Yourself

MESSAGE FOUR
Anything's True If It's True for You

MESSAGE ONE

YOU CAN HAVE IT ALL (AND YOU DESERVE IT!)

MESSAGE ONE

YOU CAN HAVE IT ALL (AND YOU DESERVE IT!)

1

How Many Buses Can You Catch at Once?

Christopher stares in shock at the note in his mail. It's from the leader of his church youth group, and here's what it says:

> Dear Christopher,
>
> How are you doing? We sure miss you on Wednesday nights. I thought I'd check and see how you are, since it's been two months since you've come to a youth meeting. We hope to see you this Wednesday!
>
> Sincerely in Christ,
> Steve

The note itself isn't shocking. It's brief and friendly, and Christopher feels good that the youth leader is checking up on him. What shocks him is finding out he hasn't been to a youth group meeting in *two months!*

Impossible! Could it really be that long? He sits down and thinks: *When was I there last? It was before football practice started, and it must have been before my car, because I remember catching a ride with Andy. Burger Haven did call me to work two Wednesday nights last month—or was it three Wednesday nights? Then there was that mini-series on TV I had to see—were those on Wednesdays too? Well, at least I'm still reading the Bible. Let's see, I last read it . . . uh . . . I can't quite remember. And I prayed back when Granddad was in the hospital . . . but he's been home for six weeks at least!*

THE CONTINENTAL DRIFT

Christopher is stunned to realize how many things have intervened between him and the Lord. While he's been busy doing lots of good things, slowly and surely his spiritual life has been doing a continental drift. Just like the continental drift, he hasn't even noticed it.

If you followed him around for a week, you'd find Christopher beginning to compromise his Christian faith in deeper ways than missing youth meetings. On the football field lately, for example, his language is sounding more and more like his teammates; he doesn't want the other guys to think he's a prissy sissy. He still gives money to the church, but even with those extra hours at work, his giving isn't increasing; the cash goes for recreation instead. And one of those Wednesday nights he missed youth meeting simply because his car wouldn't start; as a car-owner, he now assumes he can't go anywhere if his car isn't running, so he never thought of calling Andy for a ride.

Christopher isn't a bad guy! He's still a Christian and wouldn't have it any other way. So what's been going on, anyway? When and how did his sideways slip away from Christ turn into a landslide and then an avalanche?

LEAVE THE LORD? NEVER!

Well, certainly Christopher never *meant* to drift away from the Lord. Two months ago he'd have vowed he'd be in youth group forever (or at least till graduation)!

What happened?

It's really very logical. Christopher's spiritual drift is a result of what he's been listening to with the sensitive ears of his soul.

No, we don't mean rock music.

In addition to Bible studies on Wednesday nights and sermons Sunday mornings, for much of his young life Christopher has been hearing something else "preached" at him from all sides. He gets this message from television ads, school counselors, magazines, his friends, teachers, sometimes even his parents. And he believes it.

The message is this: *He doesn't have to choose between all the good things life offers him, because everything in life is rightfully his.*

YOU CAN HAVE EVERYTHING; IN FACT, YOU SHOULD!

In other words, life is a supermarket, and Christopher has been led to believe that he's pushing a bottomless cart down aisles of opportunity—with his rich uncle's credit card in his pocket. He assumes all the good things in life are available to him. Physical well-being, health, financial security, salvation, an exciting youth program, trouble-free relationships, money for college, success in school, fun, love, and happiness—they're all his for the taking. And if he finds he doesn't have one or more of the above, then life is cheating him.

Who in the world told Christopher something like that?

Lots of people. Probably some of the same people who are telling you the same thing.

He hears and sees this message of "It's all yours" in many translations. His school counselor tells him, "You can be anything you want to be! If you can dream it, you can do it!" The beer ads tell him, "You can have it all!" His coach tells him, "You don't have to settle for being less than the best!" His parents tell him, "With a good education, you can go anywhere and be anything you want!"

ALL THE BUSES AT ONCE

Our friend Christopher isn't a hypocrite. He's honestly committed to Christ and enjoys knowing the Lord. It's just that so many other enjoyable attractions are coming down the road, like one shiny bus after another, and he sincerely believes he can and should take them all. Sports, dates, work, a car—they *all* look good! So why choose?

There's the yearbook assistant editor job, which takes up hours when he should be studying, so he winds up studying Sunday nights when the youth choir practices. And there's *that girl* who doesn't care anything about God but is irresistibly attractive (not that he tries very hard to resist)—he tells himself he'll win her to the Lord by dating her, but so far they haven't gotten around to any religious discussions.

So did Christopher *mean* to lose interest in Christ? Of course not. All he *meant* to do was enjoy every good opportunity that came his way, because they're all his. He's been doing his level best to grab them all. And now he's frustrated to find out that somehow they've been coming between him and Christ.

JUMP ON THE SCALES

Of course he never weighed whether any of those attractive involvements might detract—or at least distract—from his attachment to Christ. It never occurred to him to think about that! He assumed that he could fit Jesus in with everything else in his life, or that Jesus would come along with him on all of them, or something—anyway, that it wasn't an "either-or" proposition.

ONLY ONE PIECE?

Well, who likes either-or? Nobody. Nobody wants to have to pick and choose between two good things. Getting one means not getting the other! We'd rather have the whole box of candy than have to decide between the square piece with the mysterious bulge or the round piece with the swirl on top.

Do we *have* to choose among all the things life holds out to us?

Of course we do. All the time.

First of all, we have to choose for the simple reason that we can't be everywhere at once doing everything at once. If the band and the debate team both practice during first hour, we can't physically be in both of them. If Burger Haven is open during the youth group meeting, we can't be there and at the youth group at the same time. We would save ourselves a lot of grief if we realized some of our own limitations of time, space, and energy!

WHOSE KINGDOM?

But there's another, deeper choice we're constantly making. That choice is between Christ's kingdom and the world's kingdom. We chose Christ when we accepted Him as Saviour. And like it or not, aware of it or not, we continue to choose for or against Jesus—not just once, but all the time.

Jesus said it directly: "No one can serve two masters. Either he will hate the one and love the other, or he will be devoted to the one and despise the other. You cannot serve both God and Money" (Matthew 6:24).

IMPOSSIBLE COEXISTENCE

Jesus was saying it's impossible to simultaneously serve God *and* everything else in life that clamors for our attention, time, and effort. We can't serve both God *and* work, or both God *and* social status, or both God *and* the yearbook staff or sports or drama—or anything else, no matter how good it is.

Now before you run out and resign from your job, sports, and the yearbook staff, wait a minute! The question is not what you're *doing*, but what you're *serving*. That is, who controls you? To what or whom do you devote yourself?

CHOOSING FOR AND AGAINST

Let's put the choice in human terms. In the Bible, the relationship between the Lord and His people is often compared to a love relationship.

Say you have a date and you're really looking forward to your time with that special person. At the appointed time and place, Special Person fails to show up! And when you finally make contact by phone, Special Person says casually, "Sorry, something came up that sounded like more fun."

Do you come first for that person? It doesn't look like it or sound like it. A choice was made *for* some other interesting pastime—and *against* poor you. The coin was flipped and you lost. It's obvious that such choices get made all the time in human relationships. We also continually make them about the Lord: for Him or against Him.

CONSTANT CHOICES

Our friend Christopher didn't realize that with each new involvement and interest he took on he was making a definite choice about what was important to him. And since those things couldn't all be equally important to him, when he chose to elevate some things he also chose to put the Lord further and further down the priority list.

To use that image from the Bible—the image from Jesus Himself—Christopher has been continually choosing which master he's going to serve and which kingdom he's going to live for. By putting himself in the willing service of other things, he's actually been choosing *not* to serve Jesus, or at least to serve Jesus less and less.

Let's look at that analogy of the love relationship again. Two people who are important to each other confer with each other about what they're going to do. They don't go running off in separate directions and making separate plans. When Christ is your Special Person, you ask *Him* before you decide whether to commit yourself to any activity. You check to see if your plans conflict with His plans, and you go with His plans for you.

Jesus went on to talk about how we decide

whether to trust the Lord for what we need or take on the massive burden of worrying about it ourselves (Matthew 6:25-32). The first choice is living for Christ's kingdom; the second choice is living for this world's kingdom. Choosing for the world's kingdom leads to running around, frantically trying to hold everything together; choosing for Christ's kingdom means relaxing and letting the Lord take care of our needs however He decides.

WHERE DO YOU LOOK FIRST?

Christ gave us and Christopher and everybody else a guiding rule for making sure we're living in His kingdom and not in the dark kingdom of self and Satan. Read on in Matthew 6:33: "But seek first His kingdom and His righteousness, and all these things will be given to you as well."

Seek first God's kingdom. The alternative is *not* to seek His kingdom. That choice is up to us. There will be things which contribute to God's kingship over us (and our citizenship in His kingdom), and things which don't help us live for Him. We can't expect to serve God *and* grab at everything that looks attractive; we need to ask first, "Who am I serving by serving this?"

And as you're clever enough to have figured out by now, that means disbelieving the seductive message "You can have it ALL!" Because you can't have it all—not the parts of the "ALL" which will draw you away from Christ—if you want to keep your full-hearted commitment to Him.

WAIT A MINUTE . . .

Let's get back to Christopher staring at that note from his youth leader and try to help him out of his shocked state. What could he have done to prevent his spiritual continental drift?

In the first place, he could have done earlier what he's doing now—stopping, sitting down, and thinking.

For example, when Christopher first applied for work at Burger Haven, he knew that youth meetings were every Wednesday night. He could have decided on his priorities and told his boss, "I'm not available to work Wednesday nights. At all. Period. Sorry. I have a previous commitment." Then the restaurant wouldn't call him; or if (as employers often do) they called him anyway, he'd have his answer ready. Christopher wanted cash as well as spiritual nourishment, and he tried to leave Wednesday nights open to both. He didn't foresee that the chance for the cash would actively compete with his involvement in the youth group.

Take that car too. It's like magic how car ownership transforms some people from walkers and bikers into creatures who can't budge without their four wheels. Christopher wanted a car because it meant freedom and independence. He didn't notice himself becoming *dependent* on his symbol of independence. It soon became easier to sit home when the car got contrary—letting the car run his life. How could he have gone about it differently? Well, when Christopher got that car, he could have looked it right in the headlights and said, "I'm going to those youth meetings whether you go along or not—run, walk, or crawl!" The car would not have talked back.

EASY ENOUGH

The decisions we've talked about would have been easy enough for a person firmly committed to the Lord and to the church. But when a person doesn't even realize that decisions are staring him in the face—and when, as a result, he tries to go both ways at once—it leads to the long, slow spiritual drift, if not the sudden avalanche.

Can you have everything? Wishful thinking! There are two kingdoms, and some desires fit in with Christ' kingdom—but not all of them do. Next time you hear that seductive message "It's all yours for the taking!" you'll be wise to respond to it something like this: "I'll take all that's rightfully mine, thank you, as long as it doesn't yank me away from Christ. As for the rest—the things that ask me to give up my friendship with Him—well thanks, but *no thanks!*"

2

If Happiness Is Having, What If I Don't Have?

Kelly has the formula for success right at her fingertips, along with the keyboard of her personal computer. She's taking all the computer classes her high school offers. Then she's going to college to become a programmer, with minors in management and investment banking. After college she's sure to grab a position which will enable her to pay off her considerable college loans, plus provide her with a well-furnished apartment and a car that expresses her personality.

Kelly's life plan continues: along the way, maybe in a business class in college or afterwards on the job, she'll meet the ideal man. He'll be sensitive, on the upward move in his profession, and a real looker; and his career goals will mesh with Kelly's.

They'll get married, and after building up a comfortable measure of financial security, they'll have one daughter and one son: two beautiful, perfect children who'll run laughing into Kelly's arms when she picks them up at the day-care center after work, before they go to meet Kelly's husband at a pizza place and the whole family goes to a funny movie together. . . .

ddddddkkkkkzzzzzspspspspspssltltltltltlt

Huh? Kelly wakes up from her daydream to find her fingers dragging on the keyboard, while Mrs. Crandall, her computer teacher, looks over her shoulder and comments, "*That* doesn't look much like today's assignment, Kelly!"

Well, what can Mrs. Crandall expect? Kelly is tired from all her studying and scrambling to get in extra hours on the computer. She's had to be at all the games, too, because she's cheerleading captain—the best one they've ever had, her friend overheard the coach saying (though secretly, she doesn't even *like* basketball and her legs ache from practicing that awful double jump all week). Today she's particularly worn out because she was up till all hours trying to break up with her boyfriend, who plans to be a career Navy officer and whose life goals definitely don't mesh with hers. But he's so good-looking, and she's the envy of every girl for landing him, and Kelly can't bring herself to tell him good-bye!

IF ONLY . . .

Mrs. Crandall, the teacher, smiles at the back of Kelly's head. She sees how driven Kelly is, and she understands very well—from the other side. In school she was also a superachiever who was always saying "If only I had . . . " and "If only I could. . . ." Now, at 31, she has it all. And she's tired too—from juggling all of it. All the conflicting responsibilities of teaching, keeping up with the computer world, relating to her students, loving and being sensitive to her husband and children, keeping the house looking decent, and chairing the welcoming committee at church. Sometimes she thinks she's so busy fulfilling herself that she doesn't have any time for herself anymore.

Mrs. Crandall would like to tell Kelly, "Slow down! You're so busy achieving everything that makes you happy, you're not even enjoying yourself!"

HAPPINESS IS . . .

Why is Kelly so focused in one direction?

Easy. Because she wants to be happy. And she defines happiness according to the message she hears all the time: *Happiness means getting and holding onto the best life offers in every area.* She can't imagine herself being happy with anything less than the ultimate.

WHO DOESN'T WANT TO BE HAPPY?

Everybody wants to be happy, and there's nothing wrong with wanting to be happy. In fact, there's something wrong with people who *don't* want to be happy! So maybe it would be a good idea to take a look at what actually makes people happy.

You undoubtedly have friends who define happiness the way Kelly defines it: achieving the ultimate in everything. You're even tempted to define it that way yourself, if you're living in this world where the message is out that happiness is *having.*

How true is that definition of happiness? And where does it lead if we follow it?

THE PEOPLE WHO HAVE

Now and then some famous star—of TV, movies, a sport, or some other area of accomplishment—shocks and disappoints us by voting against life. The person makes headlines by committing suicide. You can think of several cases right away, can't you? Nobody understands the person's action. They say, "How could he do that? He had everything!" or, "What could have driven her to it? She had everything going for her!"

Those are extreme cases, but they say something. They at least say that, having acquired everything, some people are still dissatisfied with life. Why? It should make us curious.

We don't have to look at suicides to see that the people who have "everything" aren't always the happy people. Susan was a high school student whose parents had gobs of money; she owned everything she could want to own. Yet in Bible study when we discussed our biggest spiritual struggles, she said her struggle was with envy. We wondered, *What could she find to envy anybody about?* But apparently she found plenty.

The people who *have* don't always have happiness. You know of other examples: "beautiful people" who get depressed, lucky people who grumble instead of enjoying their luck, achievers who are down on themselves for not achieving enough.

Look around with open eyes (and your heart open as well as your eyelids) and you'll see people who aren't happy, but who ought to be happy if the commonly accepted message is true.

It should be a caution for Kelly. Does happiness really wait for her at the end of all her success? And—what scares her the most—what happens if she doesn't succeed?

I'VE GOT IT MADE

A well-known person in the Bible had what Kelly and Mrs. Crandall both crave. He wrote, "I have learned the secret of being content." Lucky guy, huh? He had it made. He must have written those words sitting on top of a pile of cash, reading his latest press notices in the fan mags or the *Wall Street Journal*.

Well, not quite. And neither did he write those words on a computer keyboard while daydreaming of his future plans to own the ultimate driving machine. The Apostle Paul wrote those joyful words while sitting in a prison where he had been locked up unfairly for talking about Christ.

Paul wrote a lot about joy in his Letter to the Philippians. He told where and how he found joy, and he encouraged anyone reading his letter to share his joy with him.

If you jump into the Book of Philippians at chapter 4, verse 4, you'll find Paul sounding like he has it made. He has the joy all of us want, and he has so much joy that it's spilling over and he's telling his readers how they need to rejoice with him! He urges confidence and encourages people to ask God for what they need. He promises them the peace of God.

Not bad, huh? Happiness, peace, and all her needs met—that's exactly what Kelly wants. She could learn something from Paul. So how did Paul get this happiness—enough of it to have some left over for others?

JAIL-BOUND JOY

If you look back at the beginning of the Philippian letter (particularly 1:12-14) you'll find out that Paul was a Roman prisoner when he wrote those words.

Not exactly the situation we have in mind when we imagine contentment! His readers in Philippi weren't surprised to find him imprisoned for Christ, because he had wound up in prison in Philippi at the time he was first evangelizing in their area. In fact, the jailer who guarded him was very likely a member of the congregation who received this letter! (Read Acts 16 for the almost incredible story of how the Philippian church got started.)

Keep reading in Philippians and you'll see that the letter is actually a thank-you letter. It's a grateful message for a gift they had sent Paul across the miles by the hand of the messenger Epaphroditus. Now Paul was sending back Epaphroditus, who had fallen seriously ill but had recovered. He would carry back Paul's expression of gratitude, and it would find its permanent place in our New Testament.

"THANKS" DOES WONDERS

Here's the first part of Paul's secret of joy: his heart was grateful. He wasn't grumbling; he was giving thanks. He appreciated what he had, and he refused to gripe about what he didn't have.

How different from Kelly and a thousand achievers like her, who concentrate on what they don't have—accomplishments, possessions, relationships. What they do have, their latest achievements, pass quickly into the background as they strain forward to the next unacquired treasure.

PEOPLE BEFORE STUFF

Look at *what* Paul was thankful for. "I rejoice greatly in the Lord that at last you have renewed your concern for me. Indeed, you have been concerned, but you had not opportunity to show it" (4:10).

Instead of thanking the Philippians for their gift (whether it was money, warm clothes, or a box of homemade cookies) he thanked them *for their concern.* In the isolation of the prison it was not things, but people who cared, that made the difference for Paul.

OTHERS, NOT ME

Continue reading Philippians 4 and you'll learn that Paul was not only grateful for the Philippians' interest in him; he was deeply interested in them. Their relationship was a mutual commitment to one another.

Commitment is another part of Paul's secret of contentment. His heart was given over to these people. "I have you in my heart; . . . I long for all of you with the affection of Christ Jesus" (1:7-8). When you read Paul's other letters and see him expressing similar concern for all of the churches he helped start, it is easy to see why he found little time to worry about not having his freedom or not having the money to run out and buy the latest style robe. His attention was taken up with his love for people.

DEEPEST DOWN OF ALL

Yet even more important—most important of all—to understanding Paul's secret of contentment is Philippians 1:21: "For to me, to live is Christ and to die is gain."

As important as people and the needs of the churches were to Paul, his first commitment was to Jesus Christ.

It was because of Jesus that Paul first went to Philippi; he and Silas went on a mission to preach about Christ in places that had never heard of Him.

That's how Paul lived. His life was commanded by Jesus. Whatever happened to him, he could trust the Lord to take care of him and provide for him.

Paul had given over the control of his life to someone else besides himself—to God. When we do that, we aren't so pressured to demand and achieve and acquire. Why? Because it isn't up to *us* anymore to make sure our lives turn out right. It's up to God. Of course we still need to cooperate with God in carrying out His will, but we no longer have the burden of totally running our own lives by our own wits.

HAPPY NO MATTER WHAT

Paul said more than, "I have learned the secret of being content." He said, "I have learned to be content *whatever the circumstances*" and, "I have learned the secret of being content in *any and every situation*" (4:11-12). Here was a truly free person whose joy was not dependent on whether something good had just happened to him. He could have joy literally no matter what!

Was Paul only making a pitiful effort to feel better because he was in such bad shape? Like saying, "I've never had anything in life, but oh well, I'll grin and make the best of it"? No—he'd been both rich and poor. "I know what it is to be in need, and I know what it is to have plenty," he wrote (4:12). He'd been on both sides and he was the same person both ways—one who trusted the Lord and found joy in knowing Him.

THE STRENGTH COMES FROM JESUS

Paul's most joyful statement is saved for last. "I can do everything through Him who gives me strength" (4:13). Who's "Him"? Well, it's certainly not

Epaphroditus or Silas or even Paul himself; it's Christ.

Knowing the Person who made everything (us included) and who understands us completely is bound to make our lives more joyful than trying to go it alone, without Him. Once we know Him, He makes possible things we never dreamed were possible.

We'd be wrong to get the idea that Paul, with all of Christ's power behind him, was lazy and laid-back because of his ability to relax in the Lord. In his own way Paul was as driven and goal-oriented as Kelly. The difference is in what drove him, what his goals were.

OPPOSITE MESSAGES

Kelly thinks she can't be happy unless she achieves and acquires certain things for herself. Paul focused on living out God's will and doing things for God.

Kelly believes the message she hears everywhere: that happiness is in having. Paul believed the quiet inner message he heard from the Holy Spirit: that joy is in knowing God.

Ultimately, despite her dreams of a husband and children, Kelly is out to please herself rather than to live for others. Paul lived for other people and the Lord, and his reward was joy.

Kelly is at a disadvantage. The way she's going, all her happiness is up to her. She's afraid she'll be frustrated and miserable if all the good things she dreams about don't happen to her.

Once she gets connected with Christ through faith, though, she'll find her focus changing to Him instead of her circumstances. It won't matter so much whether she lands a certain job or has a certain car or house. But anything and everything is still possible.

It's even possible the Lord will let her have what she's dreaming of, and more. He may find ways for her to serve Him in computer programming or in teaching, like Mrs. Crandall. She may have that beautiful family and raise them to trust in the Lord.

And if Christ doesn't bring about those specific things for Kelly, He will bring about something even better for her. Not "better" by her previous standards of getting and having, but better by His standards of honoring God and loving people. Then Kelly will have "learned the secret of being content in any and every situation" because Christ is with her in all those situations!

3

When Bad Things Happen to Good Christians

Tom decided last summer that he's going to get what he deserves out of life. He's a talented, good-looking guy who feels good about himself, believes in God, and knows what he wants: money, a nice car, freedom, and a good-looking girl who's the envy of his social scene. He believes God is his loving Father who wants to give him everything good, and he plans to get all of it. He even circled in red the date on his calendar when he made his decision to go after everything he deserves. Now Tom looks back on that "red" day as The Day Disaster Started. If he's been getting what he deserves, what did he do to deserve this?

The week after his red-letter decision, Tom went to serve a tennis ball and felt something rip in his leg muscle. He was on crutches the rest of the summer and the first week of school. So much for football. So much for driving his car he worked so hard to earn the money for. So much for dating—somehow the girls seemed to lose interest while he was struggling along on his crutches and couldn't drive. Or maybe it's the bad mood he's perpetually in since his accident.

The tennis injury was only the beginning. Tom was so caught up in his pain—mental and physical—that he missed signing up for an important exam to qualify for a scholarship he needs. Now somebody less deserving will get it.

Tom is off his crutches now, but his leg still bothers him. He has trouble making it onto the top riser in the school choir, so the director has him standing on the front row, where he looks odd and out of place because he's very tall. The basses behind him complain they can't see the director. Tom turns around and snaps, "Don't blame me, blame God! He made me tall and He let me get hurt serving a dumb tennis ball!"

Then Tom feels guilty because he's hurt his Christian witness at school. But what can God expect after dishing out all this punishment which Tom doesn't deserve?

IS THIS FAIR?

No, what's happened to Tom isn't fair. Hundreds of other guys at school played tennis that summer and didn't get hurt. Somebody with less smarts than Tom won the scholarship. All the other choir members look like they belong where they are. People less attractive than Tom are dating the girls he wants to date. The "good things" in life are dished out very unevenly in Tom's school.

Actually, those good things always were dished out unevenly. Tom simply hadn't noticed because he'd been on the good end of things for so long. Now he's finding out how the less fortunate people live, and he doesn't like it.

What did Tom do to deserve all this? Probably nothing specific. His misfortunes weren't punishment from a vindictive God. They're things which happen to everybody in one form or another. They happen to Christians, like Tom, as well as to people who never give God a thought.

Think of some bad things which have happened to people you know. Think of some good things which have happened to people you know. (You can include yourself in both lists.) No doubt you can think of some terrific blessings which have happened to Christians, and you can think of some scarifying things which have happened to non-Christians which ought to get them thinking about the shortness of life.

On the whole, though, if you wrote down all the names and all the events, you would have a balanced mix of "good stuff" and "bad stuff" happening to the Christians and to the unbelievers. You wouldn't have a list of all God's children on the "good happenings" side vs. all the rebels on the "bad happenings" side. It would come out more or less equal, proving what Jesus said about God the Father: "He causes His sun to rise on the evil and the good, and sends rain on the righteous and the unrighteous" (Matthew 5:45).

WHAT DOES GOD WANT FOR YOU?

Why are we making the obvious point that both good and bad things happen to both saved and unsaved people?

Because it's not obvious to people like Tom or to a lot of other Christians. People like Tom have believed a very different message. It's expounded by popular preachers and writers, and it gains an ear—many ears—because it's what we all wish were true. It's what we want to hear God saying.

The message is this: *God wants you healthy and wealthy! You're a child of the King, and the King's children ought to live better than everybody else's children! God wants you to prosper more than other people in order to give Him glory and attract people to Him!*

Now there are many Scriptural promises about God's blessing us and supplying all our needs. We are called the children of God in Scripture, and Jesus promises us an abundant life.

Those are some of the truths at the base of this appealing but mistaken message. God does want to bless us. He loves us. He doesn't want us miserable. He wants to give us pleasure and satisfaction and joy.

All right so far. But certain teachers and preachers make the illogical step from "God loves me" to "As God's child I have the right to every advantage in this life, whenever I want it." And that's where Tom and many others get driven by the quest for success—and wind up bitterly disappointed.

THE CHRISTIAN COMFORT ZONE

Wouldn't it be wonderful if God in His goodness and great power protected all His children from harm? Life would be one big water slide. All we'd have to do is get saved and from there on it would be peaches and cream (make that peanut butter and chocolate, please). Plus we'd get to go to heaven, where the peanut butter must be indescribably sublime and the chocolate unthinkably divine!

If all Christians were better off than all non-Christians, who wouldn't want to be a Christian? The only people who *wouldn't* want to be believers would be masochists (people who like to suffer)—or else total dummies.

Now it's obvious from that mental list you made earlier that life doesn't favor Christians that way. Sure, some Christians prosper. So do some non-Christians. And some Christians suffer, and so do some who aren't God's children.

Life here and now is uneven and imperfect. And the Bible says that's the way it's going to stay until Christ comes back.

FUTURE PERFECTION

Perfection won't be found in this life—only in heaven, which we'll experience when we die or when Christ returns. And here's where some preachers and teachers, we believe, are mistaken. They take the promises of perfection in heaven and try to apply them to this fallen world right now. But we're not in heaven yet. We take part in many of heaven's blessings, but not all of them.

In the meantime, *this* world is marred by sin. It's a fallen world in the first place; we've never seen this earth as it was meant to be. Our own sins have disrupted our lives, and even after God forgives us, some effects and consequences of those sins continue. Other people's sins step all over us. We live here in the same sinful world Jesus chose to live in.

Long ago, a godly man named Job demanded to know, "Why do the wicked live on, growing old and increasing in power? . . . Their homes are safe and free from fear; the rod of God is not upon them. . . . They spend their years in prosperity and go down to the grave in peace" (Job 21:7, 9, 13). On the other hand, God also blessed some of his servants, like Solomon, who was "greater in riches and wisdom than all the other kings of the earth" (1 Kings 10:23). Read all of 1 Kings 10 and you'll get an idea of how fabulously wealthy Solomon was—and this was *before* his heart began to wander away from the Lord.

So the distribution of wealth and comfort, in this life, now, apparently is not directly related to how godly we are. In fact the Bible even has a lot of good things to say about God's special love for the poor and their special love for and dependence on God.

The Bible and our observations of life don't seem to agree with the "health-and-wealth" preachers' message, do they? Some preachers of the "health-and-wealth" gospel have a guilt-producing answer to that. They say that if we *are* believers and we *aren't* prospering far and above our neighbors, that means there's something fatally wrong with our faith. If we believed God enough, they tell us, we'd be as well-off as we could dream of being. If we're not getting all we want, they say, it's our fault.

FAITH FAULT?

In other words, if Tom's life is one disaster after another (which it has been since last summer), the fault is in Tom's faith. If he had believed God enough, God would have protected him from that freak tennis accident, and God would have seen to it that he got that scholarship, and so forth. Tom actually deserved all the things he thought he deserved (money, car, girl, etc.), but he didn't "believe for them" well enough, hard enough, or completely enough. His inadequate faith kept him from achieving the things God really wanted for him.

Instant guilt for sufferers like Tom! And guilt for many other people who are suffering under financial hardships or physical handicaps or family strife beyond their control.

We knew a couple who were having hard times on their farm. When they became Christians they expected the Lord to bless their farm and give them prosperity. In fact the Lord did enable them to make it farming—but just barely. They were very confused. They thought there must be something wrong with their faith, and they searched for the right formula or the right expression of faith to make God keep His promises about blessing them. When that search didn't work and the farm was still barely making it, they got disappointed with the Lord.

Meanwhile, all the farmers around them were in the same boat of hard times; the Christians were no worse off or better off than their neighbors. God was letting the couple live as His representatives in the midst of ordinary human problems, which could have given them great sympathy for others.

DOES JESUS QUALIFY?

If God wants us to live in luxury because we're His children, and if any discomfort proves we're out of His will, then there's someone prominent in the Bible who consistently failed the test. That person is Jesus.

Jesus could have been born into a palace, but instead He was born to people of modest means. He was even born in a stable because nobody would make room for Him. God was in control of all that, and God chose to have His Son come into the world under very humble circumstances. That says, right away, that God doesn't condemn being poor or going through hard times. Christ willingly became part of human deprivation and inconvenience—right from the start!

As an adult, Jesus traveled around with "no place to lay His head" (Luke 9:58). He was entertained in rich people's homes, but He also took joy in being with beggars and lepers.

Was Jesus a smashing success in His ministry? He tried to get people to hear His message of repentance and faith in God and love for one another, and many people listened to Him. But many others (even His own family) misunderstood Him, rejected Him, even thought that He was crazy or demon-possessed. The powerful people felt threatened by Him and decided to get rid of Him. One of His disciples betrayed Him and the rest ran off and left Him.

Christ willingly submitted to arrest, humiliation, beatings, an unfair trial, mockery, torture, and death. Not a very successful, glamorous, or even comfortable ending to a life of ministry! Jesus had it rough when he could have had it easy. The details of His life were in God's plan, and the Gospels clearly tell us that God didn't arrange for Christ to have the kind of "successful" life on earth which the "health-and-wealth" preachers tell us we should have.

Was something wrong with Jesus' faith? Of course not. Then why did He suffer while He was on earth? We can't totally answer that because we're not God, but the Bible tells us "we do not have a high priest who is unable to sympathize with our weaknesses, but we have one who has been tempted in every way, just as we are—yet was without sin" (Hebrews 4:15).

Because He suffered, Christ understands suffering and blesses it with His presence. When we suffer, we can approach Him for help, knowing He isn't put off by our needs. He has been through difficulty ahead of us and he goes through it with us. He takes part in our suffering.

Hanging on that cross, Jesus was anything but the picture of success, health, and wealth which some preachers tell us we should be. But was he a failure in God's eyes? No way! In those most unsuccessful-looking moments, He was purchasing our salvation and reconciling us to God. He was fulfilling God's plan and doing God's perfect will right when the whole world would have called Him a flop!

A REASON FOR SUFFERING

The chief reason Jesus suffered was to pay for our sins as the final sacrifice, toward which all the Jewish animal sacrifices had pointed. Jesus, crucified outside the city walls of Jerusalem, became like those sacrifices which were burned outside the Israelites' camp (after their blood was taken into the tabernacle as a sin offering). He gives us real motivation for enduring hard times:

> And so Jesus also suffered outside the city gate to make the people holy through His own blood. Let us, then, go to Him outside the camp, bearing the disgrace He bore. For here we do not have an enduring city, but we are looking for the city that is to come.
>
> (Hebrew 13:11-14)

As we follow Christ through this imperfect world, we can expect some suffering. In fact the

Bible assures us that we *will* suffer if we are truly following Him. For example, Peter wrote: "To this you were called, because Christ suffered for you, leaving you an example, that you should follow in His steps" (1 Peter 2:21).

Why not? He suffered too, and we can't ask to escape what our Leader went through. He's with us in everything we go through, whether at school, at home, on the job, or anywhere else.

OK, WHY PRAY?

Then is the Christian life any different from "ordinary" life? Of course it is! For one thing, we *have* a Leader who went through this stuff ahead of us, and other people don't know Him. Our sins are forgiven while other people are still trying to hide, excuse, or ignore theirs. We have the Holy Spirit within us to guide us, and non-Christians have to rely on their own wits.

If you're hurting, pray. "Prayer changes things," as the plaque on the kitchen wall says. But prayer doesn't change *everything*. Sometimes all it changes is us, making us more willing to bear whatever God allows us to go through and to let Him build our character through whatever happens.

TOM THE UNDESERVING

What about Tom, back at the beginning of this chapter, who thinks he doesn't deserve all the junk that happened to him? Well, we think Tom *does* have a problem related to his faith. But the flaw is not the quantity or strength of his faith; it's the *direction* of his faith.

Remember all the things Tom thought he deserved from God and decided to pursue? They tended to be self-gratifying and self-glorifying goals rather than goals which glorify God. They are nice things when they come as fringe benefits of living for Christ; as goals in and of themselves, they're inadequate and shallow.

How should Tom respond to what's happened to him? He can take comfort that God loves him in the midst of his imperfect, earth-bound life. And he can sympathize with and comfort other people who are living in the same unfair world. He can put into action 2 Corinthians 1:3-4: "Praise be to the God and Father of our Lord Jesus Christ, the Father of compassion and the God of all comfort, who comforts us in all our troubles, so that we can comfort those in any trouble with the comfort we ourselves have received from God."

A wise saying goes, "Be careful what you pray for; you might get it!" Radical as it sounds, it isn't always best for us to get what we want. What we think is best for us may be what's worst for us, and what God considers best for us may not strike us—at the time—as the best thing that's ever happened to us.

With even the most microscopic faith in God, we have to admit that He knows better than we do what's good for us. Once we shift our prayers from what we'd like to have to what God wants for us, we'll be on the way to living in His will and enjoying the true, real good He sends our way.

MESSAGE TWO

LOOK AND SEE, HERE'S WHAT YOU SHOULD BE

●●●●●●●

MESSAGE TWO

LOOK AND SEE, HERE'S WHAT YOU SHOULD BE

4

○○○○○○○

Why Do I Keep Having Problems?

Everything was going ridiculously well for Sandy. She was making more money than the year before, her writing was being published and selling well, she was happily teaching a teen Sunday School class, her one-act plays had been successfully produced at the local college, and she'd even been unusually lucky at fishing from our canoe in the Ashland slough. Things were going so well, in fact, that she found herself wondering when the axe was going to fall. The last several times things were going *that* well, some disaster happened!

EVERY SILVER LINING . . .

Some people go through life with a cheery, optimistic attitude, bouncing from success to success. The rest of us tend to go around with one eye on the lookout for the next catastrophe. As a witty pessimist said, "Remember, in front of every silver lining there's a dark cloud!"

Well, sometimes it does seem that good times don't last . . . or don't last long enough. How often have you been having a good time, everything going great, and WHAMMO! Someone jerks the rug out from under you!

Often the surprise intruder is a problem you've met before—maybe dressed up differently this time, but the same villain. It's amazing how often those familiar problems come back to haunt us after we thought we'd told them good-bye.

A guy tells us he's been unlucky in love—again. He asks us, "Every time I have a girlfriend, why does it end in a broken relationship and a lot of hurt? It shouldn't be this way!"

A girl suffers pain for a year and a half after her ankle is injured in a bicycle accident. Finally she improves and is without pain for 10 days—when another accident puts her on crutches again. "I'm only 16," she says to us. "Why have I had to hurt so much of my life? It shouldn't be this way!"

HAVEN'T WE MET BEFORE?

What are *your* recurring problems? You know—the circumstances you'd like to punch in the nose, if only you knew where their nose was?

When you've prayed hard and tried hard for victory over your bad temper, do you still blow up at the worst moments?

Is there a person whom—no matter how hard you try to get along with him or avoid him—you still can't stand and cut down every chance you get?

Was your acne back this morning after you thought it was finally gone forever? And did you find yourself fretting about it, even though you've told yourself a hundred times it's not all that important?

Did you just realize you haven't prayed for two weeks, after you promised the Lord you'd faithfully pray every morning and every night?

Did you glance at the next person's test answers and copy them—even though you know it's wrong—because it's a habit you've had since second grade?

REPEAT OFFENDERS

Life does its repeat jobs on us, bringing back again and again the problem situations and problem people we thought we'd gotten free of. Do we smile at it all? Maybe you do. Most people say, "Oh, no, not again! This isn't fair! This shouldn't be happening to me!"

And, in a perfect world, it probably *shouldn't* be happening and *wouldn't* be happening. But it is happening. Making us grind our teeth.

YOU SHOULDN'T HURT!

Why do we get upset when things go wrong? "Obvious question!" you say, but the answer is important. Not so very long ago, people tended to accept and expect a certain degree of suffering in their lives. Now suffering is out of style.

Everything around us, and a lot that's in us, gives us an attractive message: *Life is supposed to treat us comfortably.* You get the message everywhere, from TV ads for pain relievers to billboards for mental-health hospitals: "If you're experiencing stress and you feel less than perfect, you'd better get it taken care of right away because there's something wrong with you!"

Once they swallow the message that life should be pain-free, different people try to ditch their problems by different means. Drugs and alcohol are common cover-ups to mask unpleasant feelings. There are other ways, non-chemical but equally false, which people use to try to get rid of problems. People manipulate other people, or go on buying binges, or withdraw from others into a private world, or overeat, or indulge in sex with anyone who's willing—all to make themselves feel better when life "cheats" them by sending them the same recurring problems.

SHOULD EXISTENCE BE EASY?

Are you convinced that life ought to be a free and easy street? Then you're spending a lot of energy trying to make it that way. You're dreaming: "Once things finally work out the way I want them, once I finally get the things I desire, my worries will be over. Till then, I'm in limbo!"

And you've doomed yourself to an existence of frustrated waiting. You can see why: life *isn't* that free and easy street, and we spend (waste!) a lot of time waiting and hoping for it to get easy. Our problems become a "thorn in the flesh" which (we think) keep us from becoming fulfilled people.

A THORNY PROBLEM

We even pray to get rid of our problems. Paul did that. He repeatedly prayed to be out from under one thing in particular. Though he was a great Christian leader, he didn't conceal his struggle with his persistent difficulty. He wrote about it honestly in a letter to the church in Corinth, and his very personal struggle is part of the Bible now. Read about it in 2 Corinthians 12:7-10.

What was Paul's "thorn in the flesh"? People have wondered about it for years. The answer is, the Bible doesn't say. God in His wisdom concealed Paul's specific problem from us, and now all of us can read our own thorniest problems into Paul's situation. And we can apply his solution individually.

SOME POSSIBLE THORNS: PHYSICAL

Some interpreters think Paul's "thorn" was a physical illness, since it was in his "flesh." In particular, they believe it was a problem with his eyes. There are several other clues in the New Testament which lead us to think Paul had a vision problem (for example, Galatians 4:13-15, and the fact that Paul often dictated his letters to someone else who wrote them down).

If Paul's weakness was physical, anyone who has to live with some physical limitation can sympathize with him. Severely disabled people can feel isolated from others and cut off from "normal" activities by their paralysis or missing limbs or blindness or chronic pain. Thoughtless people may make fun of them. They long to be able to participate in the games and even the work other people do so easily. A physical disability doesn't have to destroy a person, but it is a continuing weight of frustration.

Physical problems can be smaller than blindness or paralysis and still get us down. Explosive acne, an oversized nose, hair that falls out prematurely, crooked teeth, obesity, being too tall, being too short . . . this is getting depressing! Let's get on to other things.

SPIRITUAL THORNS

Maybe Paul's persistent problem was not physical, but spiritual. Maybe something kept tempting him, and as much as he hated it, he kept giving in.

Paul? A victim of chronic sin?

Why not? The Bible teaches that we're all sinners. Most Christians, no matter how much they love the Lord, find they are subject to some particular personal sin which keeps on plaguing them. Some churches even have a name for it, calling it "the besetting sin."

We're not excusing sin, only saying that if you have a recurring sin problem, you're not alone!

What sin do you keep doing, no matter how hard you try to stop?

We're not talking about things we excuse ourselves for, like when we say, "Sure, I break my parents' rules, but if they didn't have such dumb rules, I wouldn't have to break them!" No, we mean the sin that breaks our hearts. The thing we grit our teeth and try not to do, but do anyway. And the good thing we try hard to do and can't—or don't—or won't.

Masses of Christian young people drop out of church and youth programs because they conclude they "aren't good enough." They battle sexual temptations and smoking and speeding and swearing and all kinds of other private wars, and they think nobody else in the group has those problems. If only they could see inside everybody's hearts, and if only everybody were honest. We all have our besetting sins.

THORNY CIRCUMSTANCES

Another possibility for Paul's "thorn" is a difficult circumstance. Being in prison would be such a circumstance, though Paul was free when he wrote this letter to the Corinthians. If you have some situation in your life that gets you down, but you have no control over it, you can sympathize with thorny circumstances.

Your parents divorce despite everything you do to keep them together. You have to work for a boss who's mean and unreasonable. Your teacher in a required course makes fun of your faith in front of other students. Your family is so far in debt you can barely afford Christmas presents, let alone college. A good friend is seriously ill. You have to move to a different state during your senior year. Ugh! We're getting depressing again, aren't we? It's true, though, that people your age often have to face circumstances like those, and worse.

PRAYERS OUT OF PAIN

So here's Paul, the great Christian leader, looked up to by many, an apostle, an authority. And he finds himself with a weakness he despises and can't get rid of. What does he do?

He did what we'd do: he prayed to get rid of the problem. Not just once. "Three times I pleaded with the Lord to take it from me" (2 Corinthians 12:8). The original Greek word for "pleaded" literally means Paul asked the Lord to come right alongside him and help him. Over and over.

And what happened? God heard his prayers. And God answered them. But not the way Paul expected Him to answer them. In spite of Paul's prayers, that thorn did not go away. Now that may not be the way we'd have written the script, but it's what the Bible says actually happened in Paul's case.

Was Paul "praying wrong" with the wrong words or the mistaken formula? No; when he tells us how he resolved his problem, he says nothing about improving his method of prayer. And he wasn't in rebellion against God; God was certainly with Paul and approved of Paul, using him to start the church. And God had delivered Paul from difficulties many times before. Look at 2 Corinthians 1:8-11, for example.

Still, *this* time all Paul's complaints and prayers didn't produce a cure for his chronic problem. The aspirin ads turned out to be false advertising, the relaxation techniques didn't give instant peace, the family counselor gave bum advice—the stress didn't go away.

FIX IT, QUICK!

Now that's not the way it's supposed to happen, is it? We're supposed to be able to *fix* things that are wrong. If we're unhappy (or so the message goes) we should take control of the situation and *do something.* And if one effort doesn't fix the problem, we should keep trying till we find something that works.

What would you have told Paul to do? What would most people today tell him to do?

"Pray harder, Paul!"

"Have more faith to believe for your healing!"

"Focus on the god within you!"

"Quit your job!"

"Try deep breathing!"

"Take this pill, quick!"

"Jog!"

A MIRACLE CURE

The good news is, Paul did find something that worked! It didn't work to remove the difficulty itself. It worked to change his attitude toward the difficulty. It worked miracles—not the miracles Paul had originally asked for, but genuine miracles!

How did he do it?

He didn't; the Lord did it for him.

First of all, Paul recognized how his pain (whether physical, spiritual, or circumstantial) *could be there for a purpose.*

Paul had enjoyed special revelations from God. He had gotten messages from God unlike anything anybody else had ever heard. He was being used by God to begin Christ's church. He claimed authority over the widespread new realm of young churches. And he had formerly been a man who counted on his heritage and his accomplishments for his own personal meaning and value—a good candidate for a swelled head, even as a Christian leader.

So, "to keep me from becoming conceited because of these surpassingly great revelations, there was given me a thorn in my flesh, a messenger of Satan, to torment me" (12:7).

Does that mean God punished Paul with a devastating problem just to keep him humble? Not exactly; the problem itself was from Satan. But God used Paul's tormenting difficulty to keep the lid on his pride. And Paul eventually became grateful for that.

PROBLEMS DO US FAVORS

That's one good thing problems do for us: they burn away pride by reminding us we aren't self-sufficient. A sprained ankle or a sick friend or even a *C* on a term paper tell us loud and clear that we can't do everything.

We should know we can't do everything, but we forget. All around us we hear the message that we have unlimited potential and can do anything we dream of doing. Yes, we *can* do a lot. We can do amazing things, with God's help. Then along comes the pimple on the nose the morning of the prom, and self-sufficiency turns out to be a falsehood. If we can't even fix our noses, we aren't exactly all-powerful.

WHERE ARE YOU LEANING?

Paul prayed about his problem, and of course we should always pray about our problems. Paul also listened for Christ's answer. When it came—whether through his conscience, a vision, reading the Word, or another Christian—it wasn't the answer Paul wanted to hear. But he accepted it anyway. The Lord said, "My grace is sufficient for you, for My power is made perfect in weakness" (12:9).

In other words, Jesus told Paul, "I love you, but you're going to stay weak. I've delivered you from other things, but in this case I am choosing not to deliver you from this particular problem. Instead, I want you to lean on My grace and My love, and I'll prove to be enough for you."

The Lord could have shown His power by removing Paul's stubborn problem. He chose to show his power in a different way—by teaching Paul to lean on Christ and trust Him for strength to get through it.

Paul looked for a miracle. Instead, he found Christ. He learned to depend on Christ instead of on miracles. Christ can do miracles and does do miracles, but they aren't always the ones we'd have picked for Him to do.

And that's the biggest favor a problem can do for us: it can drive us to depend on Christ. If we think we're strong, we can trick ourselves into imagining we don't need Him. But if we're weak, and know we're weak, we know how much we have to rely on

Him. Leaning on Him is a much better position than standing up straight under our own power. Our own power is temporary and will fail us, but His is forever and will never fail.

MY WEAKNESS, HIS POWER

What happens when we admit our own weakness and lean on Christ? His power shows through our weakness. "My power is made perfect in weakness," He told Paul, and He tells us too. Depending on Him, we discover we can get through things that used to defeat us. We can hold our heads up in situations where we used to have drooping chins and hunched shoulders. We can, because He can.

Paul finally became grateful for his weakness, he said, "so that Christ's power may rest on me"(12:9). Depend on Christ and you'll find yourself saying with amazement, "When I am weak, then I am strong!"

MESSAGE TWO

LOOK AND SEE, HERE'S WHAT YOU SHOULD BE

5

What If I Don't Look Like a Star?

This would be a good point in the book to give an example of a teenaged girl or guy who's striving to stay in fashion with clothes, hairstyle, accessories, preferred music, favorite TV show, and favorite activities.

The problem is, this book won't be printed till a year or so from the time it's written. In publishing, that's not so long. In styles, that's a long, long time. Any specific examples of what's "in" right now will very likely be out-of-date by the time you read this.

What a dilemma! It's the same dilemma everybody faces in trying to keep up with what's current in how you should look and act. How do you keep up with it all?

THE FASHION SIDE STEP

One alternative is not to keep up at all. Occasionally Sandy likes to dress in old clothes. Not work clothes or painting clothes—good dress-up clothes, just *old.* As in antique. It's called vintage clothing. She has '30s and '40s clothing, some authentically old from secondhand shops and estate sales, some she's made herself from old patterns. When the historic railroad depot in our town was restored and renovated into a restaurant, she wore one of her "historic" dresses to opening night.

What's interesting about wearing vintage clothing is that other people either love it or hate it. They all think it's unique, but their reactions to "unique" are quite different. Everything from "Wow, is that beautiful!" to "Uh . . . interesting shoes you're wearing."

PASSING FANCIES

Of course all our vintage clothing was new once. Long ago (or not so long ago) it was the latest. But styles change, and what was new is now old and odd. Fashions tend to run in cycles, however, and if we hang onto our old clothes long enough, they'll come back in style! (Come to think of it, then they won't be nearly so interesting!)

Fashions have always been fickle. People want the newest and the latest. People crave to know what's "now." When the Apostle Paul preached in the ancient pagan city of Athens, the people there were curious about Christ chiefly because the message was something new. The Bible says, "All the Athenians and the foreigners who lived there spent their time doing nothing but talking about and listening to the latest ideas" (Acts 17:21).

Does that sound familiar? It sounds like us, right here, right now. We want to know what's currently in so we can copy it and fit in with it.

Why? Because we like the fashion or the idea or the haircut? Sometimes. More often people want the latest so they'll look like the other people who have the latest—so they'll be acceptable and accepted.

LOOKING LIKE THE LATEST

Well, is looking good a sin? Of course not. Fashion can be fun! *Or* it can be slavery.

The difference is in how wholeheartedly we believe the message which comes wrapped in the fashion: *Unless you look and act like this, you're nobody!*

The word we get from the world is that *outward appearance* is all-important. You're no good unless you look good, the message goes. Your insides may be a mess, but if you have your outside looking right, you're still OK.

To obey this message, you have to be willing to take your orders from whoever decides what's current. (Have you ever wondered who those people are and how they got the right to tell you what you should look like?) You must be willing to check up on what you *should* wear before you buy anything.

The message swarms all over the TV screen. And the movie screen. And the video screen. And the glamour magazines and the body-building magazines. We constantly see what we're "supposed" to look like.

The image is kind of deflating because so few of us look like that! When we try to match up, it costs us big bucks in hairstyling, clothes, makeup, jewelry, and tanning sessions. And even then, somehow we never come out looking *exactly* like that celebrity we've been trying to imitate.

I'M NOT PERFECT (ARE YOU?)

One trap in all this image-chasing is that unless we're very wealthy and already naturally very good-looking, the goal of fashionable perfection is always out of reach. Because who's perfect? Who can afford what it takes to look perfect? Who has the body for it? Who has access to the right things? A few people do, but the rest of us always have to settle for being less than the ideal image of what we "should" be.

And that leads to feeling like less than you are—less than God made you. When you can't get your hair to do what it's supposed to, or you can't afford the right label on your clothes, and you're absolutely sure everybody at school is going to laugh at you—well, you can get to feeling less than somebody! If only you could look like so-and-so . . . but you can't quite. You always know you don't quite measure up.

And that's a contradiction of what God says about you. He says you're already somebody no matter how you look. He says you're accepted and acceptable in Christ. He says you measure up because Jesus has done it for you.

BY THE WAY, WHAT'S PERFECT?

Another trap in trying to be like the advertised "image" is that the image we admire and envy can easily turn into our ideal. It becomes not just something nice, but our idea of what it would mean to be "perfect."

Often the popular image of "perfect" doesn't fit (clashes, even) with what the Bible says about what's ideal for human beings—what God thinks we're supposed to be.

The image says that outer physical perfection is

everything. Too bad for someone who is handicapped or has a low IQ or suffers from hairlessness—they're out of luck by the popular standard of perfection!

In reality, despite any physical "imperfections," you're equally as valuable, loved by God, and important as the "beautiful people." But once you accept the glamorous image of what a person is "supposed" to be and look like, you're tempted to reject what God says about people.

WHO'S RIGHT?

Some Christians are very aware of the dangers of being obsessed with style. They reject the "image" of current fashion altogether and deliberately dress very plainly and simply—and out of style. In this way they show they're different from the world (non-Christians). They do a good job of displaying that they have different values. In the process, they may alienate people who are curious about Christ, but aren't ready to give up stylishness. Still, those Christians have the courage of their convictions and dare to be different.

Other Christians go to great lengths to look like the world. They believe if you're committed to Christ, you should look the sharpest and most attractive of anybody. That way you'll attract people to Christ. They don't want to participate in the world's sin, but they want to be accepted by the world. Because of their desire to be accepted, they're always walking the knife-edge of adopting the world's values as well as the world's hairstyles.

IS IT SPIRITUAL TO BE STYLISH?

Is there a "Christian" hairstyle? A "Christian" way of dressing? How long should a Christian girl's skirt be? Can a guy wear an earring and still be a Christian?

Christians come up with all kinds of different answers to those questions. And we get very emotional about our answers!

Like so many questions of Christian conduct, it all comes back to attitude. *Why* are we doing what we do?

Are we seeing ourselves, and other people, as God sees all of us? Or are we taking on the world's un-Christlike view of other people and ourselves?

SEEING ALL THE WAY THROUGH

First we have to think about how God sees us. Is He impressed with the labels on our jeans? Does He "ooh" and "ah" about our brand of hair-coloring? Is He awed if we have real rubies in our class rings? Well, we can't prove it, but we don't think so. He made everything in the universe and owns everything, so it's hard to imagine Him being impressed with anything we hang on ourselves or do to ourselves to improve our outward appearance. He puts beauty and order into the world, but He doesn't judge people by how good-looking or well-dressed they are.

There's something in the Bible that tells us what God *does* look for. It's in 1 Samuel 16.

Israel had asked for a king so they'd "be like all the other nations" (1 Samuel 8:20). (Just like us today, they wanted to imitate the people around them!) Through the Prophet Samuel, God had anointed Saul the first king, but Saul had failed in his responsibilities. Now God was sending Samuel to anoint a substitute king of Israel. God told Samuel the new king would be one of the eight sons of Jesse, but He didn't tell him which one.

Samuel got to Jesse's house and saw the first son, Eliab, apparently a very good-looking young man. Read what happened: "When they arrived, Samuel saw Eliab and thought, 'Surely the Lord's anointed stands here before the Lord.' But the Lord said to Samuel, 'Do not consider his appearance or his height, for I have rejected him. The Lord does not look at the things man looks at. Man looks at the outward appearance, but the Lord looks at the heart' " (1 Samuel 16:6-7).

LIVING INSIDE OUT

Samuel saw a tall, good-looking guy named Eliab. Eliab looked like a leader. He probably had a big open smile, a friendly handshake, a congenial but strong-minded manner. He may have bowed deferentially to Samuel and made some spiritual-sounding remark, like, "I would be greatly honored to do God's will by becoming the next king of Israel. Where's my crown?"

Samuel was all set to declare Eliab king by pouring oil on his head, the symbol of God's anointing. Eliab looked like the winning candidate with no competition in sight. There was one problem: Samuel was going by outward appearances, and outward appearances in this case were deceiving. "Don't do it!" the Lord said. "Eliab is not my man! Samuel, you're looking on the outside, but I look on the inside, at the heart."

We don't know why Eliab was rejected or why six of his brothers were rejected. Maybe God saw secret inner sins, jealousy, selfish ambition, phoniness, cowardliness—who knows? All we know is that God saw the truth where human eyes saw only the image.

The man that God picked—David—was not even

considered in the running by his father and his other brothers. Samuel had to request him to be sent in from the sheep pasture. As soon as David came in, the Lord told Samuel, "Rise and anoint him; he is the one." This same David became Israel's greatest king, a writer of many of the Psalms, and an ancestor of Jesus Christ. Not bad for a kid nobody else in the family was willing to give a chance!

PUT LOOKS IN PERSPECTIVE

Now for all of you out there who *are* good-looking and are wondering if you should wear a mask, we have to admit David had "a fine appearance and handsome features." Someone else described him as a guy who "knows how to play the harp. He is a brave man and a warrior. He speaks well and is a fine-looking man" (1 Samuel 16:12, 18).

It happened that David did have a lot going for him in the way of talent and looks. But clearly that was not why God chose him as king; his oldest brother apparently had as much going for him, outwardly. God chose David because, He said, "I have found David son of Jesse a man after My own heart; he will do everything I want him to do" (Acts 13:22).

What is God looking for? A heart that will obey Him—regardless of whether it resides in a beautiful body or a body missing limbs or eyes.

God is looking for a heart that loves—regardless of whether that love shines through a face that could grace a magazine cover or a face full of pimples.

God is looking for a heart that puts Him first—regardless of whether the wrapping the heart comes in—the body—is dressed in the latest designer rags, or literal rags from the thrift shop.

So if you happen to look good on the outside, enjoy it! But don't imagine that God likes you better or approves of you more than the people who aren't as good-looking.

SEE AS GOD SEES

Getting God's inner vision gives us a whole different perspective on ourselves. It also gives us a whole different perspective on *other* people! If God looks beyond the outward show to see the real person, so should we. We can't see perfectly as He sees, but we can try to see beyond the surface.

That means looking at other people and *over*-looking things the world tells us are all-important. For example, if you're going to search for what's in the heart of a person, you can't get hung up on the fact that she hasn't got pierced ears, even if everybody who's *anybody* has pierced ears. Sound silly? It is—and it happens. Some Christian young people once said that another girl probably wasn't a Christian because she had *four* holes in one ear and plucked her eyebrows strangely. Yes, it happens. People are judged by such trivial appearances. Reputations have stood or fallen on an earlobe. How superficial can you get?

But people do make judgments like that. And we have to live in a world where people judge us on those trivial details of appearance. It's a cruel fact of life: If you're good-looking, others are more likely to assume you're a great person, well-adjusted, and desirable to have around. If you're plain or even homely, you've got an uphill battle, because in the world's set of values you don't have as much to offer.

The church can be the place where the world's

values get turned upside-down—or, more accurately, inside-out. The church can be where people don't look at the outward things, but at the heart.

If your church or youth group doesn't look at people the way God does, you can start your own quiet revolution by beginning to look beyond the externals. Ask, "What's this person's heart like? Does he love God? Does she need to know somebody cares? Is he lonely? Does she have creative gifts the church can use?"

You'll change other people's lives for the better forever if you see them not as the world sees them—they get plenty of that in the world—but as God sees them. You'll change your own life, too, as you become more like Christ. He doesn't care about appearances; He cares about people's souls. With His help, so will you. And tomorrow's church will be different—for the better.

MESSAGE TWO

LOOK AND SEE, HERE'S WHAT YOU SHOULD BE

6

Will I Die If I Don't Have Sex?

"You haven't ever? Not at all? With anybody? What's the matter with you?"

Actually, nothing's the matter with Phil. He's a young Christian committed to living by God's moral standards expressed in the Bible. So far he's doing OK, but along the way he's not getting much help from his rushing hormones, the perfume and blue jean ads, or his peers (male and female) who nag him with comments like the one above.

When Phil started high school, he looked forward with high hopes to growing stronger in his faith every year. He expected that as he matured in Christ, temptations to sin would fade away or become easier to cope with.

Instead of giving up the fight, Phil's temptations

have brought in a fresh army! Now Phil is nostalgic for the good old easy days of being a Christian in the fourth or fifth grade, when his biggest moral struggle was whether to use his neighbor's bike without permission.

Phil finds himself up against—and swept along by—a force which drives him mentally and physically, which he both loves and hates, which brings him pleasure, guilt, wonder, fear, power, confidence, and embarrassment all at the same time. Phil is a young Christian trying to handle sex.

HAVE THINGS CHANGED?

When it comes to dealing with sex, Christian teens often feel out on their own and beyond the reach of adult help. Right? (If we're wrong, write and let us know!) You feel that adults who say, "Well, just abstain!" grew up in a whole different time and in a different world. It was easier then, you say. Teenage sex wasn't socially acceptable then. Peer pressure was against it rather than for it. The Pill hadn't been invented, or wasn't readily available. People were more inhibited. People were more religious and abided by the church's rules.

"Now look!" you say. "Everything is wide open and we're expected—even encouraged—to have sex or there's something wrong with us. You don't understand—it's not as easy as it was for you! Things have changed!"

You bet they have! Sexually, things *have* changed radically in America in this century. Nobody could deny that. The human internals—the natural physical and emotional drives—are the same as ever. What *has* changed is the degree and amount of *external* stimulation you have to deal with. It's all around you, and you've been immersed in it so long you may not even be aware of how powerful it is.

EARS AND EYES

It's no joke—if you're an American Christian teenager your senses are flooded with sexual messages and stimulation on all fronts, all day. You'd have to withdraw from our culture to get away from it entirely. Nobody is saying that you have to be a hermit to be a Christian. But you can keep your ears and eyes—and Bible!—open and become aware of the messages hitting you from all sides.

Example: music. We could discuss the rights and wrongs of popular music all day, but one thing we'd have to agree on is how heavily and overtly sexual it is. And that *has* changed. The sexual messages in music used to be veiled and suggestive. Now they're blatant and demanding. Videos add skillful erotic visual stimulation and sexual images even when the words are bland. The sexuality doesn't even sound rebellious anymore, because society has dropped the sexual restraints which music used to rebel against.

Whatever else you may say about popular music, it's obvious that a constant intake of sexual stimulation through ears and eyes, in the company of other attractive teens, has got to feed your natural desires to the screaming point.

Then there's the tube. Sex is one constant theme used to keep TV viewers watching. Those glamourous and clever characters you passively observe night after night can hardly make it through a half-hour episode without having sex or agonizing over the lack of it, even when it's irrelevant to the plot. Even the most harmless TV sitcoms have people jumping into bed with anybody, and some people jumping into bed with everybody. Sex comes very close to being shown on screen; on some cable channels it *is* shown on screen.

What does that do to you, the viewer? It shows you nightly a parade of attractive, well-dressed, successful people who talk about and practice sex as an assumed thing, no questions asked. Sex causes some complications in their lives sometimes, but nothing that can't be taken care of in 60 minutes with time out for commercials. We imitate the people we see and admire, and for millions of people those fictional, sex-obsessed characters are their role models, whether they realize it or not.

Some TV sex is flippant and funny—and in the process Christian morality is ridiculed as a relic from the dusty past. Some TV sex is somber and serious, dealing with incest or impotence—and again, a Christian view is not even considered worth mentioning. In any case, sex is always *there.* As if you weren't already thinking and wondering and worrying about it all the time, the screen adds to your obsession.

Then there are the movies, where sex is even more openly discussed—and done—than on television. Even if you're under 17 you can easily get into an R-rated movie if you go with an older person or the ticket agent doesn't care, and anyway you can always watch it later on the VCR. Even some PG and PG-13 films are open and nonjudgmental about sex.

IS SEX VALUE-FREE?

On top of music, TV, and movies, you may have "value-free" sex-education classes where exploring and experiencing sex is talked about and assumed as healthy and normal for a teenager. (Of course, not all sex-education classes treat sex as value-free, but many do, and they teach a message of their own.)

What happens when you explore valuable human sexuality in an atmosphere which deliberately fences out values? What the Bible says is treated as irrelevant—not even allowed into the room. You're left to your own instincts and hormones to tell you what to do. And that means sex winds up being encouraged, because your inner drives tell you to go ahead and there are no moral barriers to stop you.

AIDS changed all that, some people say. People don't go out and do it with anybody and everybody anymore because they're afraid of that dreaded disease. The fear of AIDS definitely has cut down on promiscuity. Still, if the restraint is fear of disease rather than morality, it's a self-serving restraint which will end if a cure for AIDS is found. There's a parallel from history: Teens used to be warned away from sex by the threat of the ultimate social shame, pregnancy (causing it or having it) out of wedlock. When pregnancy became preventable, the fence of fear was down, and "morality" evaporated—because it wasn't in people's hearts.

WHY THE OBSESSION?

It's ironic that a society which is so open about sex seems so consistently unsatisfied by sex. We live in a culture where we can do just about anything with anybody and not be condemned or even gossiped about much. If completely free sex is rewarding, we should have a very happy populace.

But what do we have? A populace who still can't get enough—who have to hear about, read about, and see sex continually, in more forms and in more imaginative ways. They're bored. They're starving.

If sexual liberty were as good as it sounds, these people ought to be happier than they are.

That discontent is plenty of evidence that unrestrained sex isn't as good as it claims to be. Still the voice is loud with many lying messages about sex: *You have to or you won't be happy. You ought to or you're not normal. You need to or you won't be a full person.* As Christians we have to answer those claims with a true view of sex from the Bible.

SEX IS NO SURPRISE

This concern with sex is nothing new. It's true that attitudes have changed so that you're now encouraged, even pushed, to do what you once would have been forbidden to do. A lot of forces are working against you in your desire to follow the Lord and stay pure. We don't envy you or downplay the opposition you face.

But we have to say that human beings' sexual drives—the natural inner compulsion and need—*were* and have always been as strong (20 years ago, 50 years ago, or 1,000 years ago) as they are within you now. Sometimes you get the impression that mankind has undergone a sudden evolutionary burst of sexual desire in the past 20 years and you're the victim of it. The truth is that people themselves really have not changed. We've always had to cope with our own sexual desires and other people's. Contrary to how you often feel, sex was not invented last week.

Research the most ancient music and art you can find, and you'll find the theme of sexual love alive and well—delighting people, disappointing them, and driving them crazy just like it does today. For that matter, listen to music and look at movies from just a couple of generations ago—the generations we think of as prudish, inhibited, and unenlightened. Sexual love is the biggest theme. Then as now, as always, sex simultaneously gave people joy and drove them to fits of jealous rage.

SEX IN THE BIBLE

A focus on sex wasn't new even in biblical times! It's hard to find a book of the Bible which doesn't mention sexual pleasure or sexual sin.

The Song of Songs (or Song of Solomon) is a love poem; the Book of Ruth is a love story. Ask pastors and Christian parents and anybody else who has to read the Bible out loud. The Bible is so honest about sexuality and about gross sexual sins that more than one pastor has stuttered reading the Scripture of the day from the pulpit, and more than one parent has skipped over some passage at family devotions.

The very few New Testament books which *don't* mention sex are the personal thank-you and greeting letters. Jesus was not the slightest bit embarrassed about talking about sex. Neither were Peter and Paul and the Gospel writers. They were talking about more than the joys of marriage too; they had to deal with sinning Christians—sexually sinning Christians.

In Paul's letters to the Corinthians you can almost hear him tearing his hair out at their flagrant immorality. Corinth was a crossroads city—wealthy, cosmopolitan, and grossly immoral—which had once held the Temple of Aphrodite (or Venus) goddess of love—where 1,000 sacred prostitutes were available to "worshipers." Every imaginable and unimaginable sexual sin happened in Corinth. The young Christian church in that city was surrounded by sin which tempted them by its overwhelming prevalence and openness. Sounds like today's world!

WHAT'S NEW?

OK—what does it mean for *you* to know that sex isn't new and that people have always had inner and outer conflicts about sex?

It means you're not alone. That's good to know because there's something peculiarly isolating about sexual questioning and guilt. We don't often hear sex mentioned in church so we think we're the only people battling this particular temptation. But in reality we're not alone.

It means that when Phil finds himself in a car with a very desirable girl and all the time and privacy in the world ahead of them, he's not a pioneer. That awful and wonderful mixed desire and doubt he feels is shared by all humanity. He has millions of fellow soldiers in this battle and fellow sufferers in this torment.

To those Christians trying to live in the midst of the temptations of Corinth, Paul wrote: "No temptation has seized you except what is common to man." There's no exception clause for sex. Sexual temptation is the common experience of all human beings. There's also no exception clause in the assurance that follows: "And God is faithful; He will not let you be tempted beyond what you can bear" (1 Corinthians 10:13).

Phil *feels* like he's the only guy who's ever wondered whether he should or shouldn't. He thinks every other guy in his situation has taken advantage of the opportunity and he's alone in having any moral restraints. That's not true. Billions of people have been in the same spot ahead of him. Over the centuries the setting may have been a Model T or a chariot or a camel saddle, but sexually it was precisely the same question arising from the same feelings.

And believe it or not, Phil, not all of those guys went ahead. And the ones who said no survived to tell the tale—though they may have told a little different tale from what actually happened!

GOOD USE OF A GOOD GIFT

In sex-obsessed Corinth, the small minority who were Christians wanted to know how they should live their sexual lives. Some thought that the Lord would return very soon and that they had no time for marriage. Yet they were surrounded by temptations. Like us today, the Christians were getting no help toward purity. They wrote and asked Paul what they should do, and part of Paul's response is in 1 Corinthians 7:1-9.

Paul's initial advice is a little startling: It's good not to marry. He did not mean it's good to skip the wedding vows and live with your mate; he meant singleness, celibacy, abstinence.

IS ABSTINENCE POSSIBLE?

Whoa! That's what everybody says *isn't* possible! That's the unthinkable length people *won't* go to, even to avoid AIDS! That's the awful, fateful question raised by the title of this chapter: "Will I die if I don't have sex?"

The answer is, yes, you will die. But not from not having sex. Everybody will die, whether they have sex or not. You may feel sometimes like you're going to die because you don't, but you won't. And when you survive, like Phil, you'll learn something. You'll learn what we quoted earlier: "God is faithful; He will not let you be tempted beyond what you can bear. But when you are tempted, He will also provide a way out so that you can stand up under it" (1 Corinthians 10:13).

There are many older people walking around, virgins, who have never married—by choice or because they never found somebody—and who have never had sex with anyone. They wanted to, but they kept themselves pure. They're leading satisfying, fulfilled lives as teachers or priests or volunteer workers or any number of other ordinary roles and they show no sign of dying very soon. They get lonely sometimes, as do married people and people living with other people. But they have full, meaningful lives.

So, is sex desirable? Of course. Is it necessary? Obviously not.

WHO'S IN CONTROL OF YOUR LIFE?

Once you get it in your head that sex is not the absolute all-consuming drive—that you can even live without it if you have to—you're a long way toward getting control over a power that would like to control you. If sex is an uncontrollable drive which we have to satisfy or we die, then we are in its power; we've become its slaves. "A man is a slave to whatever has mastered him" (2 Peter 2:19). If, instead, sex is a gift from God, subject to your will and self-control, you are free to use and enjoy it as He wants.

That's Paul's next point in his letter to the Corinthians—controlling the sex drive. Because we're surrounded by temptations to misuse sex, he says, the best thing to do is to use it in the right way by marrying and sharing this gift solely with your marriage partner. In that committed relationship there is plenty of room and time for developing and exploring sexual expression.

"That's fine if you get married and you're happily married," you might protest, "but what if you're like those people you just talked about who never find anybody?" Then your life still isn't over. You go on serving God regardless of marital status. Because you're controlling sex rather than letting sex control you, you can be free and satisfied in your situation.

MEANWHILE . . .

OK, so much for the comfort of knowing God will take care of your future sexuality. What about now when its demands threaten to take over your life? What about the date you're going on tonight or the prom that's coming up or the car ride your favorite person asked you to take next Saturday night?

What do you do when you're alone with that person and everything says, "Yes, go ahead!"

Well, don't count on your instincts and "how you feel right then" to tell you what to do, because that answer will be yes every time! The time to make up your mind no is long, long before that moment happens. Like right now.

It's funny that some of the same voices which tell you to go ahead and do whatever you feel like doing also deny your real emotions. They say you can have sex with anybody you feel like and it's fine; then they pretend that you'll have no emotional repercussions over what you've done! As if you could be intimate with a person and then have absolutely no emotional attachment with that person.

Sex is deeply emotional as well as physical. If you have had sex with a person, you have given part of yourself and taken part of another person, and your emotions are involved no matter how much you try to deny them. Sex was designed to involve our spirits as well as our bodies.

Boys are sometimes accused of being able to have sex with a girl casually and feel no emotion for her. But ask that young man how he feels if the next day the girl will have nothing to do with him, won't come to the phone when he calls, won't go out with him again, and is telling everybody what a creep he is. Are his emotions involved? Of course they are! He'd have to be nonhuman to feel no emotions about sex.

Psychologically it's impossible for you to experience sex and just walk away and forget about it as though nothing happened. If you could do that, sex would be as trivial and meaningless as a piece of bubble gum. When God created sex, He created something very important—important enough to involve our feelings at the profoundest depths.

WHY WAIT?

Are you ready for the emotional and physical commitment of sex? The equivalent question is, Are you ready to be married to that person for life? Because God intends one to be synonymous with the other.

We were talking with a young couple who had an on-again, off-again relationship. They said they had finally decided to move in together and make it last. We thought they were a beautiful couple who were right for each other, so we asked, "Why not go ahead and make it legal? Why not get married?" To which the guy replied "Uh . . . well . . . uh . . . (cough) . . . I don't think we're ready to go quite *that* far!"

They were in love, but they still wanted to leave themselves an "out." In other words their commitment was not yet 100 percent. That "maybe" in their commitment was enough to say they weren't ready for sex as God intends it. Sex means total commitment or it's only a game—a losing game.

Do you have reasons for not getting married, or not getting married yet? If so, you have sufficient reasons for not having sex, because you're not ready to make the full commitment to the other person; and without the commitment, sex becomes a selfish and destructive force in a relationship.

Control your sexual drive instead of letting it control you, and you'll find your sexuality to be the deeply satisfying part of you which God means it to be!

MESSAGE THREE

IT'S ALL WITHIN YOU—JUST LOOK INSIDE YOURSELF

MESSAGE THREE

IT'S ALL WITHIN YOU—JUST LOOK INSIDE YOURSELF

7

There's One God—and It's Not Me!

"I don't see what's so bad about that rock star. He believes in God."

The singer in question is infamous for his grossly immoral lyrics and lifestyle. Still, he says he "believes in God," and that was enough to make this Christian teen plead his cause.

Certainly it's a good thing to believe in God! Scripture says that anybody who can live in this world and *not* believe in God is kidding himself and ignoring the evidence (Romans 1:19-20). If you took a poll and asked people on the street, "Do you believe in God?" most of them would probably say, "Of course!"

But what do people mean when they talk about "God"?

They mean a lot of different things.

WHO IS GOD, ANYHOW?

People get all kinds of different ideas about who God is, from all kinds of places. Not that there are many Gods—there's only one God (Deuteronomy 6:4 makes that clear). But people can have funny ideas about who He is. We can even grow up with false ideas of God because of certain associations we had in childhood. For example:

On your wall at home there was a sentimental religious picture of people in robes gazing at a glowing spot in the heavens. So you thought, "God must be a bright light in the sky—kind of like a UFO!"

Or you remember your preacher looming behind the pulpit in his full black robes as he gave you words from the Lord, occasionally glancing sternly toward you kids in the junior choir to see if you were behaving. So you thought, "God is a tall, forbidding man up above me, and I need to be on my best behavior in case He looks my way!"

Or maybe your Aunt Jane told the story of how she "met God" at a revival meeting when she was 10 years old and was never the same again. You don't know what she was like before, because you weren't born yet, but you concluded that "God is a celebrity who makes special guest appearances, and if we're lucky, we can shake His hand and get His autograph!"

Sound silly? It is. But those ideas are no sillier than these other common misconceptions of God:

- The old man with a flowing white beard sitting on a throne suspended in puffy clouds (He looks like a nice guy, but you're afraid He'll nod off to sleep and fall off His throne);

- The huge, huge, HUGE giant whose hands are as big as galaxies (He's got the whole world in His hands, but it's awfully hard to get friendly with Him);
- Love with a capital L, the wonderful spirit of goodwill toward everybody (nice, but really just a good feeling);
- The big Santa Claus in the sky (the spirit of "Gimme!");
- The big policeman in the sky just waiting for you to make a mistake so He can drag you off to His fiery prison.

Well, we could go on and on about phony ideas of God. Why bother?

Because you're going to hear, if you haven't heard already, a lot of goofy, wrong ideas about who God is!

GOD EXPERTS

That's right. People who seem to know what they're talking about are going to tell you all kinds of things about "God." They'll use the same word you find in the Bible: G-O-D. They'll spell it the same, pronounce it the same as in the Bible. But take note. *They won't necessarily mean the God of the Bible.* And unless you know the difference, you could be fooled.

Fooled how? Fooled into thinking they are right about God, and the Bible is wrong? No, not if you know and believe God's Word. The danger of how they'll trick you is more subtle than that. It's this: if you don't know the difference between what they mean by "God" and what Christians mean by "God," you may begin to mix some of their false ideas about God with what the Bible teaches—not even seeing any contradiction.

What are some ideas of God you may have heard, or might hear in the near future?

GOD THE IMPERSONAL FORCE

A very common idea is that *God is an impersonal force which inhabits everything.*

Never heard it? We bet you have—it's been made popular by movies since you were in the first grade or so. Ever heard of "the Force"? (If those movies are your all-time favorites, please stick with us anyway, OK? Now, where were we?)

What's the famous "Force" like? It helps people in need. It's all-powerful; in any conflict, those who rely on the Force win. It's also morally neutral—in other words, it can be used by either the "good guys" or the "bad guys." Of course for the sake of the movie plots and the audience, it usually comes to the rescue of the side you're cheering for. But the Force itself is impersonal. It doesn't care about the people on either side. It helps whoever most completely learns to yield to it, good or bad.

You might say, "Come on, it's just a movie! The Force wasn't meant to be God!" But if it isn't, it's sure a good imitation! For example, it's everywhere at once. It can be called on at any time. It does what human beings can't do. It saves people when they can't save themselves. That's a very good description of what mankind through the ages has always meant when we talk about God. The Force is an ultimate power, and the movie scriptwriters were making a strong statement about what the ultimate power in the universe is like.

GOD IN THE EARTH

Another interesting idea about God is one we hear a great deal in northern Wisconsin. We live close to nature. On the shore of vast, cold Lake Superior, surrounded by national forest, next door to a slough where beaver, blue herons, bald eagles, and even loons let you canoe close to them, near two Indian reservations and a local college which specializes in environmental studies, we constantly hear this: *God and nature are one.*

It's an attractive concept. It's a reaction against the harm we've done to our environment. Humankind has done a lot to destroy nature, and many people are working hard to regain a lost respect and care for the natural world. In the process some have come to reverence nature. They worship it. They find ultimate meaning and peace in getting close to the natural world. When they see pollution or any exploitation of our northern wilderness, they feel the way you'd feel if somebody spray-painted bad language on the walls of your church: it's sacrilegious.

I'M GOD! (OH YEAH?)

You don't have to live in northern Wisconsin to hear that God and nature are one. You may have heard it put this way: "Everything there is, is part of God."

Or, "God is everything there is."

Or maybe, "You and I are part of God."

That's an idea of God which is common to the movement we call "New Age." But it's not really new. It is borrowed from the ancient Hindu religion, which goes back thousands of years and is dominant in India today.

What does Hinduism say about God? It believes God is All. In other words It (we can't say "He" because it's impersonal) is actually the same as Everything.

Let's run that past again. The message is this: *Everything is a part of God. God is All there is. All is One. Everything there is, is God.* The world, the stars, the people of all nations, the people you go to school with, the preachers, the atheists, the trees in your front yard, the tires on your car, the thoughts you think, the mosquitoes that bite you, the hamburger you ate for lunch, everything—it's all One. It's all part of God.

Sure, you look out the window and daydream during history class, and you *think* you see grass and sky and cars in the parking lot and that person you'd like to date walking along with—oh no! But actually (this belief says) those are illusions. You're really seeing God out there.

Now your eyes see your own face reflected in the window glass. "Hey, if everything is God. . . ." That's right! That means *you* are also God! Quite a thought—and very attractive if you'd love to zap a lightening bolt at that person who's walking too close to your potential date.

And you might as well zap that person—let's take this out to its logical conclusion—because if everything is One, there is no difference between right and wrong. There *seems* to be, but there isn't; it's another of those illusions. Everything you do is a manifestation of God, so everything is OK.

"Who could believe THAT?" you ask. The answer is "Lots of people." People who prefer not to think about right and wrong. The idea of "God" we've just told you about is great if you want to do things you know are wrong, because this "God" doesn't care—not about right and wrong, and not about the person you're about to knock down with that lightning bolt.

On the other hand, this "God" is also unconcerned with *your* hurts. It doesn't care if you suffer. It sees no difference between right and wrong, fair or unfair, pain or pleasure. The "God" who is "All" quite literally doesn't care if you live or die.

How do all these ideas about God compare with what the Bible teaches? We must ask that question because, for a Christian, the Bible isn't an optional extra. God's Word isn't something we can just take or leave. If we want to know who God really is, we must look to the Bible—not to our feelings or our friends or the beautiful persuasive people on TV or what we think God "ought" to be, but to His Word, which actually came from Him.

So how do these "new" ideas stack up with the Bible?

The answer is: pretty bad.

It doesn't take much in-depth study to realize that the ideas about God we've just looked at are in absolute contradiction to the Bible. Yes, even when they try to drag the Bible along with them.

Suppose you had a $20 bill you suspected of being counterfeit. In order to find out if it was phony, you'd get a real $20 bill—one you knew was genuine—and you'd compare the two. The fake wouldn't stand up to the real article.

We can do the same with ideas about God. In order to test those ideas about God we've just read—or any other ideas we hear—let's first look at the genuine article. Where do we find the truth about God? In the Bible, which He gave us and which reveals Him.

Here are some basic things the Bible says about who God is and what's He's like. (This summary will be very compressed and won't begin to say ALL that could be said, but it covers some basic truths.)

1. God exists. Obvious, but let's start there. The whole Bible assumes that there is a real God who really exists. Some Scriptures which speak specifically of His existence are Genesis 1:1, Psalm 53:1, and Hebrews 11:6.

2. There is only one God. We've already referred to Deuteronomy 6:4, which says there is one Lord; you'll read the same in Isaiah 45:5-6, 21-22, and 1 Timothy 1:17.

3. God is spirit. Throughout the Bible, God is presented as a spirit rather than something physical, and Jesus specifically said, "God is spirit" (John 4:24). God can't be held in your hand like an idol, or weighed and measured like an object in a laboratory.

4. God exists as three distinct Persons: the Father, the Son, and the Holy Spirit. These are referred to as the Trinity—not three separate Gods, but one God in three Persons. At creation God said, "Let *us* make man in *our* image, in *our* likeness" (Genesis 1:26, italics added). In Matthew 3:16-17 and 28:19 we see (or hear) all three Persons of the Trinity.

5. God is personal. He is not a "thing," an "it," a "something," or a "whatever." He is a Person, a Being. (You think of yourself as a "human being" and you think of your friends—we hope—as "human beings." Well, God is the divine Being.) Look on any page of the Bible and you'll never see God called "It," even with a capital *I*.

6. God knows things. In fact *He knows everything.* Proverbs such as 3:19-20, 5:21, and 15:3 tell about God's infinite wisdom and knowledge.

7. God thinks and plans. For example, Ephesians 1:3-12 says God had a purpose and plan for mankind's salvation "before the creation of the world." The mind of God is also praised in Romans 11:33-36.

8. God does things. Genesis 1 and 2 tell how He created the universe. The entire Bible tells how He works long and patiently with mankind; in particular, look at Proverbs 16:9, 19:21, and 21:30.

9. God is the Creator. Besides Genesis 1 and 2, Psalms 33:9 and 24:1-2 are in praise of His creating everything.

10. God is eternal. He is the creator of everything—except Himself! Romans 1:20 and Psalm 90:2 tell us He is eternal. God has always been, and He always will be.

11. God is separate from His creation. He made it; He is not part of it. Before it existed, He was around and decided it would exist, as you can read in Genesis 1:1, Isaiah 45:18, and Revelation 4:11.

12. God is here. Though He isn't one with nature, He is present on earth with us. God was with you and knew you in your mother's womb (Psalm 139). The "great policeman" myth is a misunderstanding of this truth, but the truth is that God is with us always (Matthew 28:20).

13. God communicates with us. He gave us His Word, and throughout the Bible people testify to how God spoke to them and revealed truth to them.

14. God loves. In fact He is the source of love. Read John 3:16-17 and 1 John 4:7-10. God expressed His personal love in Jesus Christ (2 Corinthians 5:19). In Jesus' life we see love in action as He dealt with hurting people around Him. Finally He died to pay the penalty of sin which God could have rightly and justly put on us. His love is the best proof we have that He is very personal and not an "It."

15. God feels. Besides love, God says He also experiences anger (Psalm 78:21); grief (Ephesians 4:30); rejoicing (Isaiah 62:5); delight (Isaiah 65:19).

16. God is holy. Angels sing of His holiness and goodness in Isaiah 6:3 and Revelation 4:8. That means God is perfect and is the source of all good. Therefore He is the *only source of moral law—He cares about how you treat other people.* The Ten Commandments which He gave (Exodus 20 and Deuteronomy 5) are an expression of His character, as is everything else the Bible calls good and right. Our own consciences tell us that right and wrong, good and bad, are real, not illusions.

REAL VS. PHONY

As you were reading these Scriptures, you were probably already mentally comparing them against those current ideas about "God," and you can already see some differences—the flaws in the counterfeits.

You have a choice which God you will believe in. People are free to decide to believe that God is a neutral Force, or God is the universe, or even that they are God! But people who call those things "God" are not believing in the God of the Bible—as much as they may claim the Bible backs them up. (It doesn't.)

Which will it be? We can't claim to believe in the God of the Bible, the personal God whom Christians worship, who made the world and came into that world in Christ, while at the same time swallowing counterfeit ideas of "God" which are against the Bible!

You can take the counterfeit $20 if you want to. But if you had a choice between the counterfeit and the real thing, which would you choose?

●●●●●●●●

MESSAGE THREE

IT'S ALL WITHIN YOU—JUST LOOK INSIDE YOURSELF

8

○○○○○○○○

If I'm Not God, Who Am I?

"Who am I?" Everybody asks that question. When you were a little kid, it was sufficient to know your own name. When someone asked, "Who are you?" you could say, "I'm Heather" or, "I'm Rob." (If your name was Lillian or David, of course, those answers wouldn't apply!) You could further identify yourself by your place in the family, such as, "I'm Kris's little brother" or, "I'm Mr. and Mrs. Fitzseltzer's daughter."

A few people are happy all their lives with such statements of their identity. Most of us want more. As we grow up, we want bigger and better answers to the question "Who am I?"

People around us are eager and willing to answer that question for us. We all want so much to be accepted as part of the real world that we listen hard for people's evaluation of us and try harder to fit in. We may hate the labels they put on us, but we tend to believe them.

"Who am *I*?" scoffs Joanne. "I'm the misfit—the person nobody likes. I'm a zero."

If you've escaped that cruel evaluation of yourself, you can be thankful, but thousands of teens don't escape it. The impression can last through adulthood.

"Who am *I*?" Brad echoes proudly. "I'm the jock—the athlete."

Great for developing self-discipline, and wonderfully rewarding as long as Brad is winning, it's also an identity which can get blown sky-high by a car accident or a broken leg that never heals right.

"Who am *I?*" sniffs Karen. "I'm the smartest student in school."

Those *A's* and scholarships are nice, but beware if you transfer to a bigger school or go to a prestigious college with people who were tops at *their* schools. You may discover you were a big fish in a very small academic pond.

SO WHO ARE YOU, ANYHOW?

We want satisfying and lasting answers to the question "Who am I?" We want to be *somebody* and we want the *somebody* we are to last longer than this year's football season.

For every God-given human hunger, the forces of deception have a rack of junk food. Remember (from the last chapter) the New Age idea that "all is One" and there is no difference between right and wrong or between you and God? If you're one with the universe and God is the universe, then you are God.

Now our own experience and common sense tell us that's obviously false. Have you walked on water lately? Have you created any suns, moons, and stars? Just as you're ready to say, "Aw, come on!" and walk away, the deceivers say, "Hold on! You just don't *realize* yet that you're God. If everything is one, there really are no limitations on you. Limitations are an illusion. Your problem is that you're ignorant. You need to start saying, 'I'm God,' and acting like you're God!"

AN OLD TRICK

If you know your Bible, you know that this isn't the first time humankind has been advised to start acting like God. The first time humankind played God was in the garden of Eden. Satan's original temptation to Eve was "You will be like God" (Genesis 3:5). Did that usher in a golden age? Of course not! It ruined our relationship with the true God and with each other, and we're still suffering from it today.

THE BIBLE'S ANSWER TO "WHO AM I?"

But New Agers are partly right, which is what makes their ideas such dangerously attractive counterfeits. You *are* terrific, and you are like God—not because you are "one with the universe," but because you are set apart from it.

If you carefully read the first chapter of Genesis, about the creation of the world, you'll be struck by a change at verse 26. Up till that point, you're reading a description of various things coming into being. God creates them, says something about their purposes, blesses them, and says they are good. Then last of all He makes humankind—and there is something different about how he approaches this new being He is about to create:

> "Let Us make man in Our image, in Our likeness, and let them rule over the fish of the sea and the birds of the air, over the livestock, over all the earth, and over all the creatures that move along the ground." So God created man in His own image, in the image of God He created him; male and female He created them.
>
> (Genesis 1:26-27)

SOMETHING NEW!

There's something different going on here, different from everything else which God had created up till this point. Never before had God referred to His own image and likeness as the "map" for something He was creating. (If you wonder why God said "*Our*" image instead of "*My*" image, the best explanation consistent with the rest of Scripture is that God is three Persons: Father, Son, and Holy Spirit, and in communicating with Himself, He can properly say "Us.")

God never said that heaven, earth, the sun, the moon, or any of the animals were made in His image. He blessed them and called them good, but He did not say they bore His own likeness. Only about humankind—you and me—did God say that.

I'M LIKE GOD? HOW?

Does that mean God looks like He could be your twin? Probably not. The "likeness" of God isn't what He *looks* like, but what He *is* like.

We cannot adequately say all that "the image of God" means. But we can make a few observations about His image and how we are made in that image. First of all, we share with God the ability to think—to reason things out and come to conclusions. We are self-conscious; that is, we are aware of our separate identities as persons who have a past, present, and future. We are creative; mankind has always had a natural ability and inclination to create things beyond bare necessity. Even cavemen had paintings on their walls! Like God, we have emotions such as love, anger, and even hatred. We are also spiritual beings with the ability to make moral decisions, choosing between right and wrong. All these things demonstrate our unique relationship to God—a relationship which animals, plants, and minerals do not share.

SO HERE WE ARE!

Those wonderful new beings, humans, now fill the earth and are dreaming of filling the solar system. One of them is reading this book right now. They are amazing creatures. They're capable of great feats of daring and imagination. They dream, plan, and love. Some of what they dream, they achieve. They built the pyramids and the Saturn rockets. Through them God's Holy Spirit even wrote the Bible.

OOPS! WHAT'S WRONG?

"Yeah," you say, "but one of those wonderful creatures called human beings stuck his finger in my face yesterday and called me nasty names in front of my friends. And another of them almost ran me down pretending he was winning the Indy 500."

Could that be possible? If humans are like God, why are they capable of being so—well, to put it nicely—*rotten?*

You can look around and see evidence that something is drastically wrong with the human race. Watch the nightly news and read the paper. All over the world people are bombing each other to settle arguments over who's right. If they aren't bombing each other, they're busy building bigger bombs and *planning* to bomb each other.

You can turn off the TV and see the flaw in humanity much closer to home. How many times a day at school do you see people "bombing" each other? People attack each other with gossip, lies, and insults. People cheat and steal, then try to get somebody else to take the blame. Walking into some high schools is like walking into a lions' den! If you're not well-liked and popular, you get the short end of everybody's jokes. Even if you *are* well-liked and popular, somebody's jealous of you and always trying to pull you down. Even church youth groups can be flawed with fighting and cliquishness.

Sometimes home isn't much better. Family members argue and compete. They may even say they hate each other.

Did God, who is wise and holy, deliberately create this bunch of selfish creatures? Was it His idea to make beings who can build the Statue of Liberty and land on the moon but can't get through a day without stabbing each other in the back?

THE FATAL FLAW

Of course not! The way people are is not the way God intended people to be. Your own common sense tells you that life is *not* perfect just the way it is, and you are *not* everything you should be.

That's a relief! You don't have to pretend everything is fine all the time or your life is faultless.

There's something wrong with how things are. There's something wrong with *us*.

That "something wrong" is sin.

AN UNPOPULAR WORD

"Sin" says different things to different people. When you hear "sin" you may think "bad movies" or "free sex" or "swearing."

Actually sin is rebellion against God, whatever form it takes, whether in thought, word, or action. Sin may look very respectable, like a wealthy all-white neighborhood which refuses to let in people of other races. Or it may be as ugly as murder.

The problem of sin got off to an early start in human history. Earlier in this chapter we asked you to read the account of Creation in Genesis 1. You don't have to read much further, only through Genesis 3, to find the account of how humankind first rebelled against God. You may think you know the story by heart, but it's good to reread it to make sure you've got the real thing sorted out from the cartoons, literature, and jokes!

What went wrong? Satan tempted Eve to break the rules God had set down. Satan called God a liar and promised Eve she wouldn't get the bad consequences God had set for disobedience. Satan promised her that she and Adam would become like God Himself. Eve made a conscious choice to listen to Satan and not listen to God. Then she tempted Adam to go along with her, and he made his own conscious choice to disobey God too.

AN INFLUENTIAL APPLE

The consequences of their brief feast on forbidden fruit were shame, fear, alienation from God, a whole new difficult way of life, and finally death.

Too bad for Adam and Eve. Too bad for their offspring: Cain, Abel, and the others. Too bad for us. The human race is fatally flawed by sin. We will never understand ourselves if we don't understand that sin is what's wrong with the human race.

The Apostle Paul explains how all of us down through the ages have been affected by sin: "Sin entered the world through one man, and death through sin, and in this way death came to all men, because all sinned" (Romans 5:12).

This is the doctrine of "original sin." We all are born with sin alive and well within us. Nobody has to teach us to do wrong; it comes naturally.

SIN IN THE NURSERY

Recently we heard some new parents express dismay that their eight-month-old son was grabbing other kids' toys and bopping the other kids—right in the church nursery! The father sighed, "I guess it just proves original sin."

It's true. Your parents tried to surround you with good influences, but even if you'd been raised in a bubble, you would still have found ways to sin.

"The many died by the trespass of the one man. . . . By the trespass of the one man, death reigned through that one man. . . . The result of one trespass was condemnation for all men. . . . Through the disobedience of the one man the many were made sinners" (Romans 5:15, 17-19). Like an invisible infection, sin has affected the human race ever since the first humans decided to disobey God.

UNFAIR!

Unfair? Of course. But before we put all the blame on Adam and Eve, we should ask ourselves, "Would I have done any better?"

If you had been tempted to disobey God—to gain power or special knowledge, to look good, and to satisfy your appetites—would you have resisted? God made humanity with the freedom to choose whether to obey or disobey Him. Maybe Adam and Eve could have remained faithful to God. But somewhere along the line of human history somebody else would probably have blown it. Maybe you. Maybe me.

So humankind is flawed and scarred by sin. We are born with the tendency toward evil, and we soon do our part to follow up on it.

GOD'S BRILLIANT SOLUTION

We humans try all kinds of things to get rid of our sin problem, even imagining that we're God and there's no such thing as sin! God did something infinitely more brilliant—and effective. He came into this sinful world in Christ and offered His own life for our own sins.

"If we claim to be without sin," the Bible says, "we deceive ourselves and the truth is not in us. If we confess our sins, He is faithful and just and will forgive our sins and purify us from all unrighteousness" (1 John 1:8-9).

We have the choice of lying to ourselves and to God, claiming we're not sinners—or confessing our true and honest state to Him and letting Him forgive us through Jesus.

NOT A SINGLE EXCEPTION

Who needs Jesus? Everybody. Because original sin affects everybody. "There is no one righteous, not even one; there is no one who understands, no one who seeks God. All have turned away and together become worthless; there is no one who does good, not even one" (Romans 3:10-12).

There may seem to be exceptions to original sin. You must know people who don't *seem* to be sinners. Maybe you're one of them. They seem to be able to claim, "I'm one with God." They are clean-living and decent; they live moral lives. They are voted Good Citizens and win Kiwanis Teenager of the Year awards. They're credits to their families, schools, and communities.

Are those people sinners? You bet they are. The Bible says that without Christ, those people are as separated from God as the gangster or the skid row bum. "All have sinned and fall short of the glory of God" (Romans 3:23). They need Him as much as a murderer does.

What's their invisible sin? It may be that they take all the credit for their goodness and don't acknowledge God—and that's rebellion against Him, because it does not acknowledge that He's the Creator and they are only creatures. Or they may be proud and look down on people of lesser achievement. Or they may simply ignore God as though He's not important.

SO WHO AM I?

So to answer our original question—who are you? You're a creation of the eternal God, and He loves you—so much that He came into this world in Christ to turn you away from evil and toward Him.

Those who give up their prideful rebellion and stop playing God will find themselves in touch with the real God, who will live with them and within them forever! All of us who know Christ can give a fearless and confident answer to the question "Who are you?" We can say, "I'm a child of God!"

9

Who's Writing the Script?

Since we work with teens and write for teens, the conversation in our house—even the adult conversation—often turns to what it was like to be an adolescent. One night the conversation got almost spooky.

"When I was a teenager I thought the world wasn't real," Dave said. "I thought I was the only one who existed, and what seemed to be out there was really all inside my head. I was making it all up somehow, or it was being made up for me, but it wasn't really there."

"I believed the same thing!" said Phyllis. "I thought everything that seemed to be happening to me wasn't really happening—it was only appearances, and I was the only thing that was real."

"Everything that happened to me was some kind of test," added Dave. "If my mother called me and said it was time to get up and go to school, that was a test to see how I'd react and what I'd do. But none of it was really happening."

Fortunately, our friends seem to have outgrown their I'm-the-only-one-who-exists philosophy. It's a good thing, because if they were right, then *we* wouldn't exist—except as some kind of "test"!

You may be thinking, "Do they have strange friends, or what?"

But we have a suspicion that similar thoughts have sometimes crossed your mind, too, when you wonder if what seems to be the world "out there" is really out there, or if you're imagining it all or making it all up. You suspect you might possibly be all alone in the universe; in fact the universe itself might exist solely inside your imaginative head.

THE RETURN OF SOLIPSISM

By the way, the idea that you're the only thing that actually exists is a real philosophy. It has a name: *solipsism.* So the idea isn't new with you or even our friends.

What *is* new to our American culture is a kind of second cousin to solipsism. It's this message: *I create everything that happens to me. Reality is only what I perceive it to be: I make my own reality.*

You may have seen a TV movie in which a star dramatizes her spiritual "pilgrimage" through just about everything except Christianity. She's standing on a winding mountain road above a cliff where several busloads of people have crashed to their deaths. Her "spiritual guide" tells her not to feel sorry for those people. They must have *wanted* to die, he says, otherwise they wouldn't have died.

We've never been in a bus accident but we've been in a couple of minor car accidents. Maybe you have too. It's a terrible feeling and the last thing you *want* to have happening to you right at that moment. So what did that spiritual "guide" (actually a deceiver) mean by his strange remark?

He meant that each of us is so completely in control of our own fate that whatever happens to us is what we *make* happen.

In other words, so the message goes, you make reality. You actually create what's real for you. Your mind and your will are so all-powerful that whatever you want to happen, happens.

Including car accidents and football injuries?

Yes, say the message-givers.

Well sure, you say. If you drink and drive, for example, you're responsible for smashing into the tree you were too drunk to see. If you're not in shape and you get hit on the football field, you're going to break your body.

But the givers of this false message mean more than that you're responsible for your foolish choices. They claim you're responsible *even for the things that don't seem to be your fault.*

You mean I make myself get laid off at work when the economy is bad? And I make my own poor eyesight and learning disabilities and stuttering and snowstorms?

Yes, they answer. You're totally responsible for your life. Whatever happens to you, happens because you want it to happen. You create your own reality, they say, and therefore your idea of reality is valid for you no matter how crazy it seems to anybody else. And other people's perceptions of reality are true for them—even if you think they're loony.

BACK TO "WHO'S GOD?"

If you skipped or dozed through the last chapter, "If I'm Not God, Who Am I?" please go back and read it now, because the message which says "I create my own reality" comes out of the more fundamental message "I am God." (Spoken by prideful humans rather than by God Himself!)

If humans are in charge of the world, then of course humans make what's real. If human beings are the ultimate reference point in the universe, then what we say goes and what we dream happens. If humans are all-powerful, then of course we determine everything that happens to us. Even the things we don't seem to be in charge of (like being the victim of a hit-and-run accident) as well as the things we obviously have some control over (like what kind of grades we make). It's a question of who's in charge of the universe.

New Age thinkers who believe in reincarnation may go so far as to say that you chose your own parents!

Could *that* be possible? Well, if human beings are God, anything is possible!

But we aren't God. He is He and we are we and the two are never the same.

WHO BELIEVES THIS STUFF?

Who wants to believe that we make our own destiny even in the seemingly uncontrollable areas of life?

For a start, people who want to be in control of life and who want to play God. Which is all of us to some degree, and some people to a great degree.

The idea that you're in charge of your entire existence has the seductive lure of personal power. If you are making your own reality, we certainly don't have any right to tell you what's real. It's even foolish for us to be writing this book to try to help you in your Christian life, because we can't teach you any truths; you're making your own truths.

The idea that you make your own reality puts you in charge (or seems to put you in charge) of your own universe. That's what Satan wanted for himself—and that's what, in a way, Satan got, though his universe was hell.

Pretending that you make everything happen gives you the aura of being a king or queen. It's a sense of power—ultimate power. It's very attractive to people who prefer to deny God's place in the universe as King.

THE CONSEQUENCES OF SOLIPSISM

Being one's own king or queen at first sounds terribly responsible. The buck stops here, with you. You can't blame anybody else for what happens to you. Anything that goes wrong is your fault, and you can take credit for anything that goes right. If you are in charge of your own reality, you seem at first glance to be a dignified person standing tall and proud over your individual accomplishments, nobly assuming responsibility for your own life.

In reality, however—God's reality—the belief that you are in charge of everything in your life leads to *irresponsibility.* Why? Because nobody in the world matters but you.

Very few scenes are more chilling than the one mentioned earlier, in which the "spiritual guide" looked down at the bus catastrophe and announced that all those innocent people really wanted to die. There wasn't a scrap of compassion for the people who had been carried to their deaths on vehicles they couldn't control. After all, if they were in charge of their lives and they died because they wanted to die, why should we feel sorry for them? They only got what they wanted.

If everybody is a little god, we can't help each other. We shouldn't even try to help each other. "Gods" don't need any help. If we try to help each other, we're intruding on each other's godness. We are each quite literally alone to work out our own fate and destiny with nobody's help. So goes the message that we make our own reality and are in charge of our own lives.

DISTORTED FACT

Like many of the other false messages we've examined in this book, the one we're looking at now has some truth mixed in with it. (A dash of truth is what makes successful lies so believable.) The truth is that we need to take responsibility for our actions, and we do have a lot to say about the outcome of our lives.

Take your grades in school. You had no control over the amount of intelligence you were born with. You went along with whatever influences surrounded you in your early childhood—how much you were encourged to learn and enjoy learning, what kind of books were read to you, whether anybody filled you with the joys of starting to count or saying the alphabet.

Then, gradually, you became more and more responsible for learning. It began to be up to you to read your assignments, do your homework, apply yourself to studying whatever your teachers were attempting to teach you. It became *your* job to fill your mind with the things you needed to learn, whether Bible study or math or computer science or the rules of a game in gym.

College or tech school or the military or employment will call for even more responsibility. It will be up to you to carry out the jobs that are given to you. How well you do them will be your decision to make and carry out.

As you've matured, your relationships have also called for ever-increasing personal responsibility. When you were two years old and your playmate hit you, you could be excused for hitting back. Now you're relating to people in a more mature way. If you have a problem with another person, you have choices to make about acting Christlike and trying to mend the broken relationship.

If you have a job, it's the same with difficulties there. If your boss doesn't like you, you can make life miserable for both of you—or you can decide to get along with your boss as well as possible and show him or her God's love. You probably can't determine who your boss is going to be, but you can do a lot toward creating a good relationship with even the most difficult boss.

Then of course there's the obvious control we all have in areas like drinking and driving, physical conditioning, diet, prayer, Bible study, caring about people, and many other areas of life where it's clear that what we do is up to us.

HOW CLOSE TO A GOD?

Can we jump from "I'm responsible for taking the initiative to be Christlike" to "I'm writing the script for my life"? No, for the important reason that the Bible says God is the one ultimately in charge of our lives.

James wrote some words of warning to those who bragged about their control over their own futures.

> Now listen, you who say, "Today or tomorrow we will go to this or that city, spend a year there, carry on business and make money." Why, you do not even know what will happen tomorrow. What is your life? You are a mist that appears for a little while and then vanishes. Instead, you ought to say, "If it is the Lord's will, we will live and do this or that."
> (James 4:13-15)

By comparing our earthly lives to a mist, James didn't mean to call us unimportant. He knew we are so important to God that Jesus died for us. Still our lives on this earth are temporary and can vanish at any time, like a mist. We should stay aware of the shortness and the unpredictability of life. And we should always remember that God, not we ourselves, is sovereign and is in control of our lives.

If we don't even know what will happen tomorrow and can't control it, how can we be God—or even little gods? We are people: fallible, sinful, imperfect, needy, created and loved by God.

GOD IN THIS WORLD

We are not gods on this earth. But there was one time when God did walk on this earth. He willingly entered an imperfect world. He did miracles here. He provided a way for us to be forgiven for playing God. He "emptied Himself" and "made Himself nothing" (Philippians 2:7, RSV, NIV). He subjected Himself to all our human humiliations except only for sin. He lived victoriously on earth, not by throwing around His Godhood, but by submitting to His Father.

When He left this earth, it didn't look radically different. He left behind His Spirit and His followers. And any time in the years since then, when one person or group has chosen to accept Him, He has shared Himself with them and changed their lives forever.

He is the one in charge of our lives. When we try to play God and run our lives by ourselves, we go against everything we were made to be—everything *He* made us to be.

OUR WORLD OR HIS?

Am I making my own reality?

Well, whose world is this, anyway? Whose reality is this that we find around us every day? It's God's reality, marred by human sin but still rightfully His.

We make choices every day, but we aren't ultimately in control of the universe. God has not left, resigned, or abdicated the throne. We live best when we live in submission to Him, not imagining we're in charge, but letting Him be in charge. Then, and only then, will we know our rightful place in the world He has made.

MESSAGE FOUR

ANYTHING'S TRUE IF IT'S TRUE FOR YOU

MESSAGE FOUR

ANYTHING'S TRUE IF IT'S TRUE FOR YOU

10

Do I Invent What's Right?

Andrea wishes that just once somebody would give her some answers.

Ever since she can remember, people have been telling her she's in charge of her own life. As a little kid she was told, "The whole world is yours, and you can decide to be anything you want to be!" As a junior higher she heard, "You have unlimited potential!" Now that she's in high school, she's hearing, "Nobody can tell you what's right and wrong for you; you have to decide that for yourself!"

Andrea's getting tired of being totally in charge of her life.

Just once she'd like somebody to tell her some definite answers. But nobody has any. Her parents seem reluctant—even afraid—to push their "old" values on her, and her teaches claim they can't tell her what's right. She has to decide those issues for herself, they say. They don't mean she has to *find out* what's true; they mean she has to *determine* what's true—"for her."

Well, it's confusing to Andrea. She doesn't know what to think. What seemed right yesterday seems wrong today and vice versa. She's kind of flattered that people think she's capable of manufacturing her own answers to the meaning of life, but when the crunch comes she'd like some dependable guidance.

A few years ago (she was told) sex was OK with anybody anytime as long as you both felt it was OK. Now that everybody's scared of the dreaded disease AIDS, peer pressure suddenly says it's "right" to be prudent and stick to one "safe" partner. There are other examples of the ever-changing world of morals. Drugs used to be in and now in some schools they're not; drinking used to be out and now in many schools it's in.

"How am I supposed to know what to do?" wails Andrea—silently, only to herself, because it's not OK to beg for rules and guidelines. "If what was right yesterday isn't right now, what's it going to be next week? What *am* I supposed to do?"

Andrea has a legitimate complaint. Young people like her are asking, "What's my life all about?" and many adults are boldly replying, "Boy, I dunno!" Or else they're answering, "I know what *my* life is about, but I don't have the right to push that on you so I'll keep my mouth shut!"

WHO KNOWS WHAT'S RIGHT?

Does anybody know what's going on?

Do the people who know what's going on have

any right to tell anybody else?

Andrea tries to live by the creed she's been taught: *You make your own right and wrong.* It leads her into complicated situations.

Her friend offers her some stolen test answers in advance of an important test in Mr. Flipperman's math class. "I know how much you want to go to college," says the "friend," "and you need good grades, and Flipperman is such an awful teacher you'll never get an *A* out of him without a little help." Andrea accepts the answers and tries to quiet the nagging voice inside her which says she shouldn't do it. After all, she does need to go to college and needs good grades to get there, and if Flipperman weren't so unreasonably difficult she wouldn't have to cheat in the first place.

Then another "friend" offers her the answers to another of Flipperman's tests which the first friend wasn't able to get hold of. But this time the arrangement is different: this "friend" is not offering to *give* Andrea the answers, but to *sell* them to her. Andrea balks. "That's not right!" she says. But she's not sure why. The money makes it feel dirty; cheating felt nicer when it was a favor, not a business deal. Besides, she can't afford it this week.

Is Andrea confused? Of course. That's a very small sample of the uncertainty which plagues her every day. Not knowing what she should do, she does what feels best at the moment, subject to change without notice.

WE ALL WANT RULES

We humans love freedom, but we also crave limits and guidelines. We want somebody to tell us how far we can go in all directions. Left to ourselves in absolute freedom, we feel insecure and unloved.

Yes, unloved. Suppose you ask your parents how late you can stay out Friday night, and they say, "It doesn't matter; come in whenever you feel like; we won't hear you anyway because we won't be paying any attention; dawn is fine." How do you feel? Your first thought may be, "Ah, freedom!" but then you wonder how much they really care about you if they're that uninterested in you. If they don't care enough to wonder why you're not in at 5:00 A.M. and to worry about whether you've had an accident or have been held up by highway robbers or have a flat tire in a thunderstorm, do they care about you?

You may protest and complain about your parents' rules, but there's security in having rules. They lay down those rules for you because they care what happens to you. That's love—imperfect like all human love is, but definitely love.

Even those who insist that we should make our own rules for ourselves and shouldn't shove our rules on each other wind up formulating surprisingly rigid rules for themselves—and for others.

The old rules about how to behave on dates may be out, but does your school have a set of its own "rules"? Can you date more than one person at once, or is that "two-timing"? What's permissible for a couple to do on a first date? How about a second date? Your school or your social group undoubtedly has unwritten (but well-known) rules about boy-girl relationships, and people stick by them. If they don't keep those rules, they risk disapproval from peers.

LOOKING FOR LIMITS

In our anything-goes society, people appear desperate for rules. Cult-like groups are springing up around self-proclaimed leaders who promise to tell their followers how to think, how to relate to others, how to live. People accept the most outlandish claims of self-made "experts" on the meaning of life, the reason for our existence, whether we've had previous lives, whether we're going to have a future life, and what we should value.

Others are resorting to deceptive psychics and mediums to tell them who they are and what they should do with their lives. And they *believe* these foolers, going on faith without requiring evidence or proof.

Why are people flocking to anybody who can give them answers? Because they don't have any answers themselves, and their souls cry out for answers. They want to know why in the world they're here and what they should do while they're here.

GOD HAS ANSWERS

It doesn't surprise God at all that we people crave guidelines, limits, boundaries, and answers. He made us this way. We're created by Him to respond to Him and live the way He wants us to live. Adam and Eve originally knew that and lived God's way, till they decided to go against Him—and we've been going against Him ever since. But we still have the inborn need—which He gave us—to find our security in Him. To find Him. We weren't made to live alone spiritually, inventing our own rules for life. We were made to live with and for Him.

All through the Bible, God tells us how much we need Him. Not because He's "imposing His values on us," but because He made us and understands fully that we can't live without Him.

In Isaiah's time He said,

> I am the Lord, and there is no other. I have

> not spoken in secret, from somewhere in a land of darkness. . . . I, the Lord, speak the truth; I declare what is right. . . . And there is no God apart from Me, a righteous God and a Saviour; there is none but Me. Turn to Me and be saved, all the ends of the earth; for I am God, and there is no other.
>
> (Isaiah 45:18-19, 21-22)

Does that sound like God is crudely pushing His ideas on human beings who would be happier if they were totally free? No, it sounds more like God is pleading with us to come back to Him because He's our only hope.

That's the situation—to use human language—in which God finds His creation: He created us and knows what's best for us, but we rebel and invent our own rules for living, and then we even say that nobody has the right to impose any rules on us!

DOES GOD COME AND GO?

Have you ever been told, "If you believe in God and in Christ, that's fine for you, but God doesn't exist for me"? Or something along those lines?

We've been told that many times. Recently we were attending an environmental lecture on endangered animals. In the middle of an otherwise fine talk about preserving wildlife, the naturalist posed the question of why it's desirable to save endangered species. She said, "Some people want to save these endangered animals because the Creator made them and they're part of His creation." (Fine, right?) Then she went on, "And *that's valid for some people.*"

Now that's an illogical way of looking at God. He's the Creator of the world—"for some people" but not for the rest of them? If they don't believe He created them, then He didn't?

If God created the world and everything on it, then He created the world and everything on it. If He didn't, He didn't—there's no halfway point where He's the Creator "for some people" but not for others.

If God is real, then He's real. No one can wish Him away. He can't be be "real" for me and simultaneously "not real" for you. A "god" like that wouldn't be God at all; He'd be a phantom or a piece of wishful thinking.

The same kind of mixed-up messages are tossed around about right and wrong. "The Ten Commandments are valid *for you*," we're told, "but not for me." "Christ's dying on the cross for you is real *for you*, but for me He's only a legend." And so forth.

WHO GAVE GOD THE RIGHT TO BE RIGHT?

Every Christian living in this mixed-message culture has to answer the question, "Are God's laws for everybody or only for me and my church?" If you're wishy-washy on that answer, your witness will never be strong because you won't really believe you have the right to tell anybody else about the Lord—and you'll secretly wonder if God is only a piece of your own wishful thinking. Once you confidently answer, "Yes, God is God for everybody!" then you'll have confidence in Him and in what you believe.

What does God Himself say about all of this?

"Before Me no god was formed, nor will there be one after Me. I, even I, am the Lord, and apart from Me there is no savior" (Isaiah 43:10-11).

"I am the first and I am the last; apart from Me

there is no God" (Isaiah 44:6).

"You are my witnesses. Is there any God besides Me? No, there is no other Rock; I know not one" (Isaiah 44:8).

"I am the Lord, who has made all things, who alone stretched out the heavens, who spread out the earth by Myself" (Isaiah 44:24).

Powerful statements by a powerful God! We've been quoting a few gems from a whole field of truths God says about Himself in Isaiah 40–45. He wants people to know that He is the only God. Because He's being egotistical and pushy? Hardly. Because He knows people need Him, and He wants us to know Him. He wants to enter into a relationship with us, mending the damage of sin, reconciling the sinful rebels to himself. That's why Jesus came. When God offers us that relationship and reconciliation, He tells us outright that He's the only way.

He boldly asks those who doubt Him: "Who has understood the mind of the Lord, or instructed Him as His counselor? Whom did the Lord consult to enlighten Him, and who taught Him the right way? Who was it that taught Him knowledge or showed Him the path of understanding?" (Isaiah 40:13-14)

Good questions! Who did all that? Nobody! The Lord doesn't need anybody to tell Him what's right. He already knows. He *is* what's right. He makes the rules for us from His own character, and that's what's best for us.

ARE CHRISTIANS INTOLERANT?

In our enthusiasm for sharing our faith with other people, Christians are often accused of being too narrow. We say God exists and Christ died for us all and we need to accept Him—truths we strongly believe are for everybody. Some people insist we should be open-minded enough to let other people have contradictory views.

Of course, we need to accept people as they are, for Christ has accepted us. However, we don't need to believe everything they believe or tell them that their beliefs are fine even if those beliefs are wrong. God desires for them to know the truth—often through the witness of us, His people. Not by being pushy, but by being bold in love, confident in Christ.

Are we intolerant? Yes, we're intolerant of falsehood and phony messages. Yes, we get impatient with people who are stubbornly set against God, whose lives could be better if they would look at Him. We're no more intolerant than some of the non-Christians who condemn us; they can certainly get very intolerant of Christians, especially when we express our slant on politics or education. Both "sides" could stand to listen to each other more and try to understand each other better.

But when it comes to the truth of Christ, we can't back down or pretend He doesn't matter.

The God we know is the real God. Let's never be apologetic about Him, because while we're apologizing, people are grasping for guidance and certainty. Despite their pseudo-tolerant words, they crave the knowledge of what's true and good and right. We can show them Christ, who is the truth, who is all good, and who is everything right.

MESSAGE FOUR

ANYTHING'S TRUE IF IT'S TRUE FOR YOU

11

Does It Matter What People Believe?

A car came out of the alley and crossed in front of Sandy as she walked along a side street near downtown. She knew the driver; he waved at her, drove on, then suddenly braked and backed up. He looked serious as he rolled down the window.

"Did you hear about Jerry?" he asked.

"No, what about him?"

"He died last night of a heart attack."

Sandy was stunned. Jerry was 39—her age. He was a popular high school English teacher who, with three other teachers, had a band that played classic rock and roll. Several years ago he had courageously confronted and beaten his alcoholism. Jerry's students complained about how hard his classes were, but they still liked him. "He'd look at me over his glasses," said one of the weeping teenagers at his funeral, "and he'd tell me, 'You can do better. You can do better.' And I did."

Jerry was something else besides a popular English teacher, a musician, a successfully recovered alcoholic, and too young to die. He was also an agnostic.

A what?

An agnostic is different from an atheist. An atheist believes that there is no God. An agnostic, on the other hand, is a person who says *we can't know* whether or not there is a God. The agnostic looks around at the world and decides, "There's not enough evidence to say if God exists." Though he doesn't actively *deny* God like the atheist, in the end the agnostic doesn't actively *believe* in God either.

VARYING BELIEFS

We have another friend, one we know much better than Jerry, who does believe in a God of some sort. Robert was a preacher's kid, but now he's drifted away from church and the Lord. He lives a devotedly independent life by himself in a cabin in the woods; he has a big garden and a few animals and makes his living doing odd jobs. We see Robert often and he knows well where we stand with the Lord. In two years of friendship he has opened up only one time to talk about his beliefs: he thinks there's something out there greater than we are, but he doesn't think it's the God of the Bible. So far, that's been the extent of the discussion.

And then there's our younger friend Mike, who was very involved in a Christian organization in high school. He says he still believes in Jesus and has a relationship with God. But Mike's outward behavior shows no evidence of faith in Christ. He recently moved in with his girlfriend, and he knows that if he gets serious about Christ, his lifestyle will have to change. So right now, for Mike, Jesus is on the shelf.

DOES IT MATTER?

Though we never got to know Jerry well, we're very fond of Mike and Robert, and we have other independent friends like them. They could never be accused of failing to have beliefs. Their beliefs are strong. You can easily see that their beliefs don't agree with the Bible, and they wouldn't argue with you about that. They are (or were) doing their own thing their own individual ways.

Does it matter?

Jerry seemed happy, and so do Robert and Mike, most of the time. Does it really matter that their beliefs don't agree with God's Word?

Sometimes we almost wish it didn't matter. It would be easier to comfort ourselves that all these guys are OK. And they aren't exactly swinging the door open wide to talk about faith and life.

Maybe you share our tremblings when you think of approaching somebody like Robert about the Lord—somebody who needs Christ but who keeps the door to that part of his life tightly shut. When our independent friends would rather not think about Jesus and they let us know it, that's intimidating. Add to that intimidation the fact that we constantly hear that everybody's truth is "right for them," and we're tempted to believe a common message: *We don't have the right to tell anybody what's true*—no matter how sincerely we believe it and how much they need to hear it. We get intimidated into silence. Christ means so much to us, but we tell ourselves, "He means a lot *to me* and that's all I can say. Maybe He doesn't have to mean a lot to my friend or my teacher."

Why rock the boat by introducing Christ into the conversation? Why risk rejection by trying to witness?

IT MATTERS!

Mike and Robert are still alive and well, and we always have the hope that they'll start to think about Christ again and come back to Him. In that hope we tend to tolerate their mistaken or rebellious beliefs for now.

But something about Jerry's death puts the whole question in a different perspective.

After living on this earth for 39 years, Jerry still claimed he hadn't seen enough evidence that there is a God. Does that matter?

With all respect to Jerry and his students and family, yes, it matters.

Why? Because despite what atheists and agnostics say, there *is* a God. Because God made this earth which (Jerry said) doesn't bear enough signs of His creation. Because God makes certain claims on the lives of Robert, Mike, Jerry, you, me, and everybody else. And because what happened to Jerry might happen to any of us, any time.

SELF-DECEPTION

Why do our friends have wrong beliefs? Why doesn't everybody worship God and accept Christ?

In the first place there's the sin which necessitated Christ's coming. "The wrath of God is being revealed from heaven against all the godlessness and wickedness of men who suppress the truth by their wickedness" (Romans 1:18). They don't suppress the truth of God by their ignorance or lack of education; they suppress it by their sin. They try to push it down out of sight and out of mind.

But God won't give up, and His truth prods at our consciences. Then, in order to shut out His voice, sin turns into self-deception. Concerning those people who suppress the truth, Paul went on to write: "Their thinking became futile and their foolish hearts were darkened" (Romans 1:21).

"The heart is deceitful above all things and beyond cure. Who can understand it?" said Jeremiah (17:9). Our hearts deceive ourselves and other people. We say we're OK without the Lord, while we aren't. Still God tries to get through to us.

GOD WHO'S REALLY THERE

God has gone to great lengths to show us that He's real. The Apostle Paul wrote, "For since the creation of the world God's invisible qualities—His eternal power and divine nature—have been clearly seen, being understood from what has been made, so that men are without excuse" (Romans 1:20). David wrote, "The heavens declare the glory of God; the skies proclaim the work of His hands" (Psalm 19:1).

The world says something: it says God made it. It wouldn't be here if there were no God. The fact that we're here, living and choosing and loving, shows that we're made in God's image (Genesis 1:27).

And the Bible says it bluntly: "The fool says in his heart, 'There is no God' " (Psalms 14:1 and 53:1). Read the rest of those psalms and you'll get a frightening picture of mankind without God. Having Him in our lives, or not having Him, makes a world of difference—now and forever.

A DIFFERENCE . . . FOREVER

Our independent friends really do need Christ. Because Jesus is not only for the here and now. He died to save us from the natural *eternal* consequences of sin: separation from God forever. If we neglect accepting His forgiveness, the natural consequences of sin still stand.

Of course, there are also advantages to belonging to Christ here and now. The peace, guidance, and forgiveness we receive from Him each day would make being a Christian attractive to anybody. But we also have observed that Robert, Mike, and Jerry are relatively cheerful about their lives even minus Christ. He wants to do more than add to their earthly happiness quotient. They *need* more than that.

We didn't say it; the Bible said it: "Man is destined to die once, and after that to face judgment" (Hebrews 9:27), and "How shall we escape if we ignore such a great salvation?" (Hebrews 2:3) There are eternal consequences for how we decide the questions about God's existence and Christ's mission on earth.

Jesus Himself said it: "What good will it be for a man if he gains the whole world, yet forfeits his soul?" (Matthew 16:26) Read Jesus' words in John 5:24-30 and you'll find an unapologetic promise and warning: He will give life to the people who have believed in Him, and there will be condemnation for those who have refused Him. Salvation is not automatically for everybody. "Yet to all who received Him, to those who believed in His name, He gave the right to become children of God" (John 1:12).

What's our message, then? Condemnation? Of course not; our message is salvation—the mercy Christ offers sinful people. That quote from Hebrews 9 about dying once and facing judgment is right in the middle of a hope-filled paragraph which explains how Christ "has appeared once for all at the end of the ages to do away with sin by the sacrifice of Himself. . . . Christ was sacrificed once to take away the sins of many people" (Hebrews 9:26, 28).

To everybody, including the people who don't want to think about or worship God, Jesus offers forgiveness by paying for their sins on the cross. That's good news worth giving out to everybody.

HOLY NERVE

Yes, it's scary to witness to people who don't want to think about God right now—or ever. God has a comforting response to our inhibitions: "For God did not give us a spirit of timidity, but a spirit of power, of love and of self-discipline" (2 Timothy 1:7).

Christ may not mean much to those people now. But Christ *wants* to mean a lot to them—yes, even to those people who aren't thinking about Him. In fact He wants to mean everything to them.

After giving His life for us, it matters to Christ whether we do anything about accepting His offered forgiveness. Redeeming us wayward humans has been a long, difficult, and costly ordeal for God. It meant blood, pain, and death for Him. He has committed Himself to saving us. So yes, it matters; it matters very much—to Him and to us—whether we respond to that invitation or ignore it.

When we realize how much God has done for human beings, we get bolder about telling those human beings what He's done. He did it not just for human beings in general or in the abstract, but specifically for Mike and Robert and Jerry. And for each of your friends who would rather not think about Him right now.

He loves them even while they're ignoring Him, or denying Him, or saying they don't know whether He exists or not.

THE BOTTOM LINE

It matters very much what I believe. It matters very much what your friends believe, and unless you exclusively hang out with all Christians (and we hope you don't), some of those friends have wrong beliefs. Not just wrong "for them," but wrong; against reality, against God who is really here. And those wrong beliefs have consequences now and forever.

"There is a way that seems right to a man, but in the end it leads to death" (Proverbs 14:12). That would be a chilling statement if we didn't know Jesus died for us; it's chilling enough knowing how many people are still at the "seems right" stage.

Should we rock the boat when people insist that they're OK? "All a man's ways seem innocent to him, but motives are weighed by the Lord" (Proverbs 16:2). "All a man's ways seem right to him, but the Lord weighs the heart" (Proverbs 21:2). The boat is worth rocking because the people who think they're OK are worth saving; and they may be on a route leading to destruction, in this life or in the next.

WITH GENTLENESS AND RESPECT

But let's rock the boat gently. Peter wrote to Christians who were "strangers in the world" (1 Peter

1:1), surrounded by non-Christian influences and outright persecution: "Always be prepared to give an answer to everyone who asks you to give the reason for the hope that you have. But do this *with gentleness and respect*" (1 Peter 3:15, italics added).

As frustrated and impatient as we may get with people who don't pay any attention to Christ, we need to love them and treat them as people God loves. We'll be most Christlike if we do that, because He was a friend to sinners.

Pray for our friends and we'll pray for yours, that God will show them He is real and that it matters very much whether they believe in Him.

●●●●●●●●

MESSAGE FOUR

ANYTHING'S TRUE IF IT'S TRUE FOR YOU

12

○○○○○○○

Who Cares about the Past—or the Future?

Jackie knows Christ, but she's rebelling against her parents' rules about what kinds of boys she can date, where she can go, and what she can do for fun.

Her dad and mom explain that they're concerned about Jackie's future. When they see her going with a guy who's not a Christian or riding around in cars with show-off drivers, they're scared. They care about what kind of guy she marries, whether she picks up bad habits, and whether she gets out of high school in one piece. They try to explain their concern for her.

"But you don't understand," Jackie replies, "I don't think that much about the future. What I care about is right now."

A certain boy is fun now for Jackie to be with. What difference does it makes (she thinks) if he doesn't believe in God? She'd never get serious about him or want to marry him . . . or would she?

Homework is boring right now. Jackie is making poor grades in some of her classes, but so what? A grade is only a mark on a piece of paper, right? Who's thinking about a record that will follow her forever?

NOW IS RIGHT NOW!

Well, what about it? Does *later* make any difference if all that matters is *now?*

Clearly the answer is "Of course not!"—*if* all that matters is now. That's how Jackie and many other young people (as well as some older people) live: for this moment, whatever day it is, whatever time of day it is on their watches now—that's reality. They don't give tomorrow a thought, much less next year or old age. As for what's past, that's even less of a concern; the past is dead and gone. So their creed is the Philosophy of the Present Tense, and their motto: *Live now before it gets away!*

NOTHING WRONG WITH THE PRESENT

There's a lot to be said for right now.

If you're a Christian, you can know for sure that God has directed you to the spot you are in—right now. God has overseen and led the ways of your life up till this moment, whether you've always been aware of it or not. Your nationality, race, age, and sex are the result of His careful planning for you.

There may be details of your life which are the result of sin or mistakes, and they may make you wonder whether *God's* hand has brought you to where you are now. Some things about your life may have come about because of rebellion rather than God's will. Say you lost a foot in a car accident as a result of your own careless driving. Or you have to go to court next week for stealing on a dare. Or you couldn't graduate last year because you goofed off and failed half your classes.

Still it's true that God has superintended your life to bring you to this moment. And this moment is a moment you can meet God—right now. He's here. He knows your condition. He's been there with you even through the mistakes, trying to get through to you. He can turn those past mistakes around for good in your life if you give Him a chance.

Right now is the only immediate moment you have to connect with God. Pick up your Bible, pray, and obey what He's telling you to do right now before it's gone!

IS THE PAST ALIVE?

Even as you pick up that Bible, however, you're acknowledging that there's much more to life than right now.

The Bible isn't being written now. Yes, it's always current and applicable to now. Otherwise there'd be no point in studying it now—except as a historic document. The Bible is *already written*. It's *history*. It records God's dealings which *have happened* (as well as how God deals with us now and what He'll do in the future).

A lot of what God has done, He has also directed people to write down. Why? So other people could read it in the future.

For example: Paul wrote about the Israelite ancestors going through the Red Sea and the wilderness, seeing God's miracles yet rebelling against

Him. Paul added: "These things happened to them as examples *and were written down as warnings for us*" (1 Corinthians 10:11, italics added).

When God did His miracles and disciplined the ancient Israelites, He *did* it in the "right now" for them. They saw it happen when it happened. But He *wrote it down* in the books of Exodus, Leviticus, Numbers, and Deuteronomy for "us," who weren't even alive then.

What's even more interesting about the 1 Corinthians passage is that when Paul said, "us," he meant himself and the Corinthians of the first century A.D. But who's reading Paul's words? We are! Now. At the end of the twentieth century A.D.! Paul's written words about God's written words in the Old Testament have now become God's additional written words in the New Testament—and Paul probably had no idea his letter would become part of the Scriptures.

God builds on the past. He gradually built the Bible out of inspired writing over a period of 1500 years. He gives His Word to us now—right now; a collection of treasures from the past, yet as current as today's newspaper.

PICK UP A PENCIL, PROPHET!

No wonder God told Habakkuk the prophet, "Write down the revelation and make it plain on tablets so that a herald may run with it" (Habakkuk 2:2). No wonder Christ told John the apostle "Write, therefore, what you have seen, what is now and what will take place later" (Revelation 1:19). And no wonder that toward the end of his Gospel, John wrote: "Jesus did many other miraculous signs . . . which are not recorded in this book. But these are written that you may believe that Jesus is the

Christ, the Son of God, and that by believing you may have life in His name" (John 20:30-31).

God wanted His works written down so people would know Him and believe in Him. The written Word is evidence of what God has done; therefore it becomes evidence of what He can do and will do.

The Lord cares about the past because He has shaped it. It's His work. He was there. For Him the past is not dead. "Jesus Christ is the same yesterday and today and forever" (Hebrews 13:8) and "With the Lord a day is like a thousand years, and a thousand years are like a day" (2 Peter 3:8). For God, the past is now, living and vital.

It was in the past that Jesus died for us. His crucifixion is a true historical event which actually happened. The replicas we put on the walls of our churches are only symbols of the real cross—which was actually there and on which He actually died. Past tense. "It is finished" (John 19:30).

HEY, IT'S HISTORY!

As a young person Sandy wasn't very much interested in the Bible, but she was very interested in history. One day she idly took a black Bible off the shelf and opened it, expecting to find lists of laws and wise sayings. She must have opened to one of the Gospels. She can't pinpoint now what it was, but her eyes fell on a straightforward narrative statement like "And Jesus went from there into Galilee." She can still recall her feeling of shock. The Bible was *history*! This was an account of something that happened! Hey, this book was *real!*

GOD OF THE PAST TOO

God was present in the past. That's comforting and reassuring to know anytime we regret *our* pasts and wish we could erase them. God was there through every shameful and embarrassing mistake we made, and He didn't stop loving us. He can redeem all the bad things which have happened to us, as well as the bad things we've done, and He can use them for good for our own growth and for helping others in similar circumstances.

God has other purposes in our knowing history; He wants us to learn from it. If we're familiar with what people have already done wrong or right, we can imitate their successes and avoid their mistakes. History can be a life-saving warning. If we don't pay attention to it, we may make the same mistakes (or worse) that previous generations made. "These things . . . were written down as *warnings* to us," Paul said (1 Corinthians 10:11). We don't simply appreciate what God did in the past; we learn from it. Our futures can be different when we look at what the church has done right or wrong in the past, what made nations rise and what made them fall, how Christians stayed faithful to the Lord, or how they got off track and what brought them back to Him.

WHEN WAS THE CIVIL WAR?

But what's happening? From all around you, you're getting the message that the past doesn't matter.

Many teachers and parents are shocked at how little history you're learning in school. Some young people don't have any idea when the Civil War took place, who was fighting whom in Vietnam, or even in what century the Great Depression occurred. History seems increasingly unimportant.

Sure, some of it is because those things happened before you were born, or at least before you were aware of them. But it's too bad when the gigantic happenings of the world's past (99 percent of which just happened to have occurred before you were born) are dismissed as irrelevant.

The "now" moment we're in right now will soon be history. With an appreciation of the past, the value of this moment will stay forever.

WILL TOMORROW EVER COME?

Then there's the flip side of the Philosophy of the Present Tense: Tomorrow doesn't matter either.

Here's where Jackie shows her disdain or at least her complacency. She says, "Who cares about tomorrow when I've got all I can do to live today?"

In one way, being nonchalant about the future makes more sense than being nonchalant about the past. You at least *know* the past and can look at it and study it thoughtfully; but who can see the future? It's an unknown you can't sink your teeth into. Why not ignore it, then? So goes the reasoning.

From a different angle, it makes far *less* sense to be flippant about the future than about the past. The past has already happened and you can't change it. The future, on the other hand, is wide open in front of you. You're walking straight into it; what happens there happens to you. You may shape the future or it may shape you, but one way or the other you are intimately involved with it.

Why then do so many people not care about the future?

THE BIG BOOM

One loud anti-future message you're getting is in the shape of a mushroom cloud. Maybe the future isn't even going to happen. If they drop the bomb, nothing will matter anyway, so why bother thinking about a future which will probably never come?

Here's where a sense of history (earlier part of this chapter!) helps. No matter what you're told, the feeling of the impending bomb is not new to your generation. The bomb isn't a new excuse to write off the future.

Young people in the 1950s also grew up in the shadow of the bomb. It was an earlier, smaller bomb, but according to our understanding it was going to cause the end of civilization. Most of us didn't expect ever to reach adulthood, any more than the current generation expects to. But we were mistaken. We did grow up. The bomb never came out of the skies, and the decisions we made and the habits we formed stuck with us into adulthood, affecting us far more profoundly than the bomb which never came.

If we think the future may not get here, and we take that as an excuse to goof off now, we may get surprised. The future may arrive and catch us unprepared. If she doesn't stop running and start thinking, Jackie in our example may soon find herself in the present tense married to the wrong person and looking bad on her job applications, all because she never thought ahead to the future.

We're not belittling the bomb. The threat of war is real and scary. A far better response than "Who cares anyway?" is to try to change that scary future to one where peace among nations is a reality. The same is true for people who use crime, corrupt politicians, AIDS, or a collapsing economy as their excuse for not caring about the future.

If you don't like what the approaching future looks like, then work to change it! If you ignore it or just let it happen, you can't complain about any unpleasantness it sends your way.

WHO KNOWS, ANYHOW?

Another reason people give for not caring about the future is that it's so unpredictable. You can't prepare for any jobs because the job you'll probably have hasn't been invented yet. Technology is changing like lightning. Today's skills are out-of-date tomorrow. Morals change week by week like hairstyles. Who can get ready for the future when you don't even know what it's going to look like?

There's some truth in that thinking. God has arranged our minds so that we don't know the future. (He could have done it in reverse, you know: made us so we know everything that's going to happen, but can't remember anything!)

The Bible, however, gives a different perspective on the future. "What has been will be again, what has been done will be done again; there is nothing new under the sun. Is there anything of which one can say, 'Look! This is something new'? It was here already, long ago; it was here before our time" (Ecclesiastes 1:9-10).

Human nature doesn't change; nobody has ever invented a new sin, just a new way of doing an old one; and God's mercy continues to be extended to human beings, who still need it. It's true that undreamed-of technologies may transform your world, but God can handle that. The fact that the future is unpredictable is no reason to become flippant about it.

THE GREAT FUTURE EVENT

All the reasons just mentioned for planning for the future are valid for just about anybody. Christians, however, have a special interest in the future and a special reason to look forward to it eagerly.

Near the end of Jesus' life on earth (a historical

event!) He told His disciples, "I will come back and take you to be with Me that you also may be where I am" (John 14:3). Again and again the New Testament affirms that Christ will return—not to be crucified again, but to reign forever.

Jesus promised His second coming long ago. In each generation of Christians some have expected Him to come in their lifetime. So far they've been mistaken, but their anticipation was biblical, because Christ taught that we should all be always watching and expecting Him.

The fact that He hasn't come yet makes some people scoff. Unafraid to deal with the issue, Peter quoted them: "Where is this 'coming' he promised?" (2 Peter 3:4). Peter went on to explain that the Lord delays not because He has forgotten us or is lazy, but because He wants to give us time to repent. "The Lord is not slow in keeping His promise, as some understand slowness. He is patient with you, not wanting anyone to perish, but everyone to come to repentance" (2 Peter 3:9).

The Lord has continued to be patient over the nearly 2,000 years since Peter wrote that letter! A long time? Too long to be true? In God's eyes, says Peter, the wait has been like only two days.

But Christ will come. The promise of His coming lifts Christians' eyes out of the present, good as it may be, and into the future. The future will count because Christ will be in it, and some part of it will contain His coming to earth again.

If that isn't something for people to look forward to, what is?

IN THE MEANTIME

What do we do while we're waiting for Christ to come back? We could spend our time staring at the sky and holding our breath. Peter had a better answer: "You ought to live holy and godly lives as you look forward to the day of God and speed its coming" (2 Peter 3:11-12).

The most appropriate way to spend our time while we're waiting for the Lord to return is to live each "now" moment the way He wants us to live it: obeying Him. Jesus said it this way in a parable: "Who then is the faithful and wise servant, whom the master has put in charge of the servants in his household to give them their food at the proper time? It will be good for that servant whose master *finds him doing so* when he returns" (Matthew 24:45-46, italics added).

Jesus wants to find us waiting for Him—but *doing* something while we're waiting. He wants us to spend this in-between time serving God and people.

We don't know how long the in-between time will last. However long or short it is, we can fill it with meaning by making the most of the time.

The promise is sure:

> For the Lord Himself will come down from heaven, with a loud command, with the voice of the archangel and with the trumpet call of God, and the dead in Christ will rise first. After that, we who are still alive and are left will be caught up together with them in the clouds to meet the Lord in the air. And so we will be with the Lord forever. Therefore encourage each other with these words.
>
> 1 Thessalonians 4:16-18

And with those words we also encourage you, as you finish this book and as you look forward to a future spent forever with Him!

MORE GREAT BOOKS FROM SONPOWER

Caution: Christians Under Construction by Bill Hybels. Build your relationship with God using the tools in this book. It will help you work on your self-image, friendships, perseverance, and more. Textbook **6-2759**

Hot Topics, Tough Questions by Bill Myers. Discover the Bible's answers to your hardest questions. Find out what God says about sex and dating, the media, the occult, and other important topics. Textbook **6-2517**

Heroes and Zeroes by Terry Powell. Want to be a hero? Learn from the successes and mistakes of real people like King Josiah, Jonah, Apollos, and Jesus Christ Himself. Textbook **6-2570**

Jesus: An Eyewitness Account by Bill Myers. Take a life-changing look at Jesus through the Gospel of John. Get the inside story on what He did *then* and what difference it makes *now.* Textbook **6-1606**

Leader's Guides with Multiuse Transparency Masters and Rip-Offs are available.

SonPower® Youth Sources

Buy these titles at your local Christian bookstore or order from SP Publications, Inc., Wheaton, Illinois 60187.